EXPRESSING
A NAZARENE IDENTITY

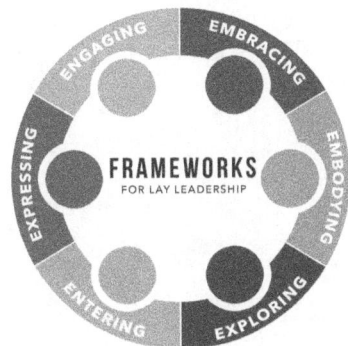

FRAMEWORKS
FOR LAY LEADERSHIP

ENGAGING · EMBRACING · EMBODYING · EXPLORING · ENTERING · EXPRESSING

Rob A. Fringer, series editor

EXPRESSING
A NAZARENE IDENTITY

Floyd T. Cunningham

Global Nazarene Publications

Dedication

To the Peru North District, which kindly invited me to lecture on Nazarene Identity.

ISBN 978-1-56344-879-9

Global Nazarene Publication
Lenexa, Kansas (USA)

TABLE OF CONTENTS

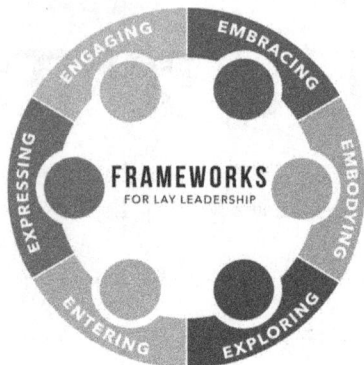

FRAMEWORKS
FOR LAY LEADERSHIP

Scripture tells us that believers are "a royal priesthood" (1 Peter 2:9). This means that all Christians, in one form or another, are called into places of ministry and leadership. Not only is this a great privilege, it is also a great responsibility. Men and women desiring to serve in church leadership in some capacity undergo basic training to assure that they understand the foundations of the Christian faith and of our Nazarene identity. This includes a deepening knowledge and appreciation of Scripture, Theology, Ministry, Mission, History, and Holiness. *Frameworks for Lay Leadership* is a series of six books designed to do just that—equip lay leaders for ministry in the Church, whether local, district, or general. These books have the greatest impact when they are read, processed, applied, and contextualised in partnership with a qualified mentor.

Welcome to this journey of transformation!

ENGAGING THE STORY OF GOD

EXPLORING A WESLEYAN THEOLOGY

EMBODYING A THEOLOGY OF MINISTRY AND LEADERSHIP

ENTERING THE MISSION OF GOD

EXPRESSING A NAZARENE IDENTITY

EMBRACING A DOCTRINE OF HOLINESS

FOREWORD

Frameworks for Lay Leadership is a series of six books designed to equip laypeople in the Wesleyan-holiness tradition for ministry and leadership in a local church. The Church of the Nazarene defines a "church" as:

Any group
that meets regularly for spiritual nurture, worship, or instruction
at an announced time and place,
with an identified leader,
and aligned with the mission and message
of the Church of the Nazarene
can be recognized as a church
and reported as such for district and general church statistics.
(Nazarene Essentials)

This definition is grounded in biblical theology as well as the practice of the Early Church. Being a church should not be confined to a particular kind of building, or any building at all. Churches can meet at any time and at any place. In our context of the 21st Century, this definition of "church" should encourage and release laypeople to live out their own callings and gifts. That is to say, church leadership is not restricted to ordained clergy. From the beginning, God has used both women and men, young and old, educated and uneducated, rich and poor to carry out his mission in the world.

The Manual of the Church of the Nazarene (paragraphs 503-503.9) makes provision for qualified lay ministers, both male and female, to serve in ministerial leadership under the supervision of a pastor and church board or a district superintendent and district advisory board. However, before this can take place, lay ministers must clearly understand who we are, what we believe, and some of the practices that guide public ministry.

Nazarenes from the beginning have been known for theological tolerance. Two maxims capture this spirit, "In essentials, unity; in non-essentials, liberty; and in all things, charity" and "If your heart is as my heart, give me your hand." It is important, then, that lay ministers understand our core beliefs and distinctions (non-negotiables such as our theological understanding of God and scripture, our Wesleyan-holiness emphasis, and our ordination of women) as well as those areas where we may embrace various interpretations and opinions (such as the form of baptism, our understanding of how God created the universe, divine healing, the nature and timing of the Second Coming of Christ, and church structures).

Frameworks for Lay Leadership is designed to guide laypeople through a validated course of study in order to lead a variety of ministries in the Church of the Nazarene. This is particularly helpful in contexts where there are no ordained clergy to plant or lead new congregations or oversee existing ones. Upon completion of this course of study, under the guidance of an ordained Nazarene minister, a certificate of lay ministry may be issued by a local church board or a district advisory board.

John Moore
Regional Education/Clergy Development, Asia Pacific Region
Field Strategy Coordinator, Australia/New Zealand

CHAPTER 1

INTRODUCTION

The Emmaus Road story (Luke 24:13-35) provides a metaphorical image of how Christ has been walking and talking alongside his Church for these two thousand years, pointing his disciples through Scriptures, to himself, and, one hopes, of how the Spirit of Christ has been walking and talking alongside the Church of the Nazarene during its 100-year plus journey. Christ joins us on the road, as part of his Church, teaching us about his Kingdom, correcting us, and making his presence and his Word known to us.

As we walk, we grow in our understanding of Christ, his Word, his Kingdom, and in what it means for us to live as Christians in the world. The Holy Spirit remains a creative presence in the Church. We are still listening to him. As H. Orton Wiley was writing the church's official theology over a span of twenty years (1919–1940), he said he was, "constantly discovering new truth, and each new discovery demanded a place in the plan of the work."[1] Similarly, one of our General Superintendents, William Greathouse, wrote that though John Wesley was the "chief architect of the doctrine of entire sanctification," Wesley did not give the "final and complete formulation of this truth." Theology, said Greathouse, is an "ongoing process; it endeavors to interpret truth in language and thought forms relevant to each succeeding generation."[2] Christ has been teaching more and more about himself and his relationship with the Father and the Holy Spirit, all the while driving his Church back to the Scriptures—not to a new revelation but to himself.

That is to say, the Church of the Nazarene is still on a journey—a collective spiritual quest. We do not have all the truth, or all the answers for which men and women quest in the twenty-first century. That is good. Women and men are searching for a church that is on a journey with Christ, for a church that will hear their questions and walk alongside them in pursuit of answers.[3]

DISCUSSION QUESTIONS

1. In what ways has Christ walked alongside you in your journey? In what ways has he walked alongside your local church? How can you share these stories?

2. Why is it important to "constantly discover new truth"? How are you working these new truths into your existing understanding about God?

CHAPTER 2

HISTORY AND IDENTITY OF THE CHURCH OF THE NAZARENE

To understand the Church of the Nazarene, we start with a look at our history. The church is the product of a work of God's Spirit that began with the revivals of John and Charles Wesley in Great Britain in the eighteenth century and continued around the world. Nineteenth century Americans considered the continuation of this Wesleyan revival a *holiness movement* within the existing churches. Like John Wesley, the holiness movement desired to revive the churches by emphasising the sanctifying grace of God within us and in the midst of us, and thereby to bring moral reform to the nations.

The Unification of Many Holiness Movements

The Church of the Nazarene declares that it was officially organized as a denomination in 1908. However, its roots reach back much earlier than that. The Church of the Nazarene brought together several geographical strands of the holiness movement. The first General Assembly of the Church of the Nazarene, which occurred in October 1907, in Chicago, brought together the Church of the Nazarene–founded in Los Angeles in

October 1895—and the Association of Pentecostal Churches of America. By 1907 the Church of the Nazarene had work in Calcutta, India, as well as churches scattered between Los Angeles and Chicago.

Prior to the Chicago Assembly, in April 1907, Bresee met with members of the Association of Pentecostal Churches of America at the Utica Avenue Church in Brooklyn. The Association was mainly comprised of churches in New York and the New England area of the eastern coast of America, the oldest of which had started in 1887. Twenty years later, these churches in the East had established missions in India and the Cape Verde Islands. At the Brooklyn church—a mission surrounded by slums, squalor, and sin—Bresee spoke to leaders of the Association of "the importance of Christianising the Christianity of America as a basis for reaching the unchristian heathen in foreign lands." When a committee on union brought back a favourable report, the minutes recorded shouting, singing, waving of handkerchiefs, and weeping for joy. The two bodies affirmed their essential oneness in doctrines. As a form of church government, they agreed on a democratic system beginning at the congregational level, and a limited superintendency, the purpose of which was to help organise churches and to care for existing ones. The assembly sang "Hallelujah, Amen," and then marched triumphantly around the church.[4] With subsequent unions and accessions, the Church of the Nazarene was to include a congregation in Ashton-under-Lyne, England, that began as the Old Cross Mission in 1874, and work begun in 1877 by Methodist missionaries in Washim, Maharashtra, India.[5]

The merger was the culmination of years of debate and prayer as to whether it was best for holiness people to remain in older denominations or to organise separate churches. There were alternatives. Both the Wesleyan Methodist Church and the Free Methodist Church were established before the American Civil War in protest of the toleration of slaveholders in the Methodist Episcopal Church. These two denominations were part of the same holiness movement—also called the *Wesleyan-holiness movement.* They were confident in the immediate sanctifying work of the Spirit both personally and socially. However, the Wesleyan Methodists and Free Methodists became, in the minds of many, too aligned with the Northeastern section of America and with the Republican Party (one of two major political parties in America). Furthermore, at this time, as prospective Nazarenes perceived it, superintendents of these good-hearted, holiness brothers and sisters were too strictly organised to embrace all of the dynamics of a restless, national movement. As well, some holiness people wanted nothing to do with anything "Methodist," even Wesleyan or Free Methodist. At the time, the Free Methodists prohibited musical instruments in worship, and this did little to endear them to many holiness people.[6]

The Church of God Reformation Movement presented another alternative. In the 1870s, D. S. Warner beckoned like-minded holiness people to "come out" of their respective denominations, which, he said, by their very nature, represented the divisiveness of the Church. He called for the unity of believers in a church made up only of born-again believers. The Church of God desired to restore New Testament practises and rejected organisational structures, including any superintendency. The "beautiful fruit of perfected holiness," Warner wrote, is unity, and, in turn, "the one all-important, and absolutely essential attribute of the divine church" is holiness.[7]

Yet another alternative was provided by one-time Presbyterian pastor A. B. Simpson, who in 1887 formed the Christian Alliance and the Missionary Alliance (which merged in 1897 to form the Christian and Missionary Alliance). Simpson stressed a four-fold gospel: justification, sanctification, healing, and the pre-millennial Second Coming of Christ. Simpson taught sanctification as a work of grace subsequent to justification, but, unlike the holiness movement, taught that sanctification was the suppression of sin rather than its cleansing. Simpson's emphases spread widely. The four-fold gospel influenced holiness missionaries such as Charles E. Cowman and Lettie Cowman, and, from there, the churches of the Oriental Missionary Society that they founded. Pentecostals later adopted the four-fold framework, modifying the point on sanctification to include tongues-speaking as the sign of Spirit baptism.[8]

The Nazarene founders' rejection of these alternatives gave shape to the church's identity and polity. The church followed the National

Holiness Association, which began in 1867 as the National Camp Meeting Association for the Promotion of Holiness, whose leaders feared any other emphasis than holiness. Its leaders remained loyal to the Methodist Episcopal Church, for which they prayed for revival. Those who attended a general holiness conference that met in Chicago in 1901 expressed their single-minded attention to holiness rather than to secondary doctrines such as healing and the Second Coming. They admonished holiness people "to avoid come-outism with all its evils," and, "as far as practicable to unite with some other evangelical church; and, where that is impracticable, to make such other adjustment as may seem, under the guidance of the Holy Spirit, to be wise."[9]

John Wesley once had written that God had raised the Methodists "not to form any new sect; but to reform the nation, particularly the Church; and to spread scriptural holiness over the land."[10] The same could be said of many holiness people. Just as Wesley advised his followers to attend to the ordinances of the Church of England in order to have the moral right to reform it, so leaders of the National Holiness Association admonished leaders to stay within the older denominations. If holiness people remained in the old churches, they would provide an influence for good within them. However, by 1901, certain holiness leaders had been put out of the older churches for preaching holiness. Others decided to leave on their own.

Increasingly, holiness leaders gave up on the idea that it would be best for those committed to the holiness message to remain in older denominations. They perceived that a spirit of worldliness, a desire for fashionableness, and social position had overtaken the old churches. Robert Lee Harris, a Southern holiness leader, lamented that the church had *backslidden* and decided it best to leave. "Would it not be better for all parties," Harris asked, "for those who believe and live alike, to come out from those who oppose them, and unite in a harmonious congregation?"[11] Independent congregations and regional holiness associations sprang up. Holiness people came together in Chicago in 1907 and Pilot Point, Texas, in 1908 out of frustration. They perceived that the holiness message was being repressed and that there was a lack of spiritual power among the older churches. They desired a conservation of the message and greater consolidation. After Harris's death, his wife, Mary Lee Harris, led the New Testament Church of Christ that he had started, which was mostly rural congregations, to become part of the Holiness Church of Christ, one of the groups that formed the Church of the Nazarene in 1908.

Unlike the New Testament Church of Christ, the Association of Pentecostal Churches of America and the Church of the Nazarene in Los Angeles were both urban-based movements. Phineas Bresee, who founded the Los Angeles based Church of the Nazarene, and Association leaders such as William Hoople, who began ministering to outcast persons in Brooklyn, New York in 1894, foresaw the need for "centres of holy fire" in American cities from which the message of holiness would spread to the world. Bresee's Church of the Nazarene, which had moved in 1906 from a large wooden structure known as the "glory barn" into a substantial brick church with stained glass windows seating 1,500, had missions among Spanish-speaking and Chinese people in Los Angeles. The Church of the Nazarene in Upland, California, included a ministry to Japanese migrant farmers. Bresee believed that the major denominations lacked the will to evangelise the "great masses of native and foreign peoples." He desired to provide a church that would include those on the margins of society. Bresee said, "I would rather have the thousands of the poor coming around the cross than to have all of the gold of the rich."[12]

From the beginning, Bresee and the other holiness groups that came to form the Church of the Nazarene allowed women full rights of ministry. An Indian woman, Sukhoda Banarjee, led the church's Hope School and Hallelujah Village in Calcutta. For Bresee, the urban and social aspect of the work in Calcutta fit perfectly the mission of the church.

Curious visitors came to Bresee's church in Los Angeles to hear the loud and spontaneous "amens" and "hallelujahs," as well as to see men and women become so blessed that they could not help but shout, stand, raise their hands, wave their handkerchiefs, laugh, and cry for joy. One would not find such spontaneous spirituality in the staid established churches around the corner. Nazarenes also sought to establish "centres of holy fire" where the purifying and empowering Holy Spirit of Pentecost would descend upon God's people. In the midst of it, Bresee decreed: "We seek no attraction, we want no attraction; by the grace of God we will have no attraction but the salvation of Jesus Christ."[13] There was no speaking in tongues, because early Nazarenes considered tongues an "outer manifestation" that could not satisfy the soul.[14] Yet, what Nazarenes sought was Pentecostal, but in their own sense of the word. Bresee stated that, "People who have the precious, satisfactory experience of Christ revealed in the heart by the Holy Spirit, do not hanker after strange fire, nor run after every suppositional gift, nor are they blown about by every wind of doctrine."[15]

In spiritual expression, early Nazarenes valued order as well as spontaneity. When Leslie Gay, in Bresee's congregation, would anticipate the climax of a sermon, and begin to shout "amen" or "hallelujah" before the point had been made, Bresee admonished him, "Not yet, Brother Gay, not yet, until I have made this teaching clear." Then, after a few minutes, after he had finished expounding the scriptural text, and God's Spirit had come, Bresee allowed, "Now, Brother Gay, you may shout." The walls of the church would reverberate with the people's great audible affirmation of truth.[16] It was more than emotion. Women, men, and young people repented and found Christ as Redeemer and Sanctifier, the life-transforming God, a mender of broken lives and homes. The saints went on to perfection. Not because of anything but God's marvellous and wonderful presence descending upon his people, they went out unashamedly to witness to their neighbours. Inviting parishioners into the experience of entire sanctification, Bresee preached: "Only the heart that is melted with the most intense love, that is heated with divine fire in the furnace of the most holy affection, is in condition to be a channel of the holiest and fullest love to [women and] men."[17]

Nazarenes aimed toward a balance between doctrine and experience. A holiness church was one in which members lived out their theology. "The Church of the Nazarene did not have its origin so much in an effort to establish a doctrinal truth," said Bresee, "as in the experience of truth already recognized."[18] He preached, "There is more religion in feeding the poor, clothing the naked and healing the sick, when it requires a sacrifice of time and money to do so, than in ebullition of the emotions, or than in all the sentiment in the universe."[19] Holiness jostled against formality and worldliness in the church, and poverty and injustice outside of it. "Men and women of pride and place, who scorn the drunkard, and who gather your robes about you in the presence of a harlot, your pride, your worldliness, your hatred to holiness, is as soul-destroying as what to you are the viler sins of your sisters and brothers." Bresee admonished: "From the heights of your pride, and social position and larger possibilities, you sink deeper into ruin."[20] That spoke a prophetic word to the rich and a dynamic love that shattered the pretences of both reclusion and moral smugness—either of which would have been for Bresee evidences of sin rather than holiness. This is to say that for early Nazarenes, a people filled with the Holy Spirit would burst forth from the church just as the disciples had at Pentecost, with the message of salvation on their lips and the marks of his purifying love in their lives, demonstrating their inward transformation through outward compassion. A Spirit-filled church went to the poorest of neighbours, to street corners and slums, to the "highways and byways."

The Association of Pentecostal Churches' work in India, which began in Maharashtra in 1898, reflected similar ideals of holiness and the holistic mindset of the missions of that day. Missionaries desired to lift up men and women in every conceivable way. They sought to change practises that denigrated women and to provide medical care, education, and relief for children and families devastated by famine. Meanwhile, back in America, Association leaders counselled churches "to cultivate the missionary spirit" and to conduct meetings "for the spread of Scriptural holiness in neglected places, remembering that the fostering of home missions means the feeding of foreign missions."[21] Strong local congregations and pastors made up the Association and there was no overall superintendent. However, for the sake of expanding the work, one energetic former Methodist minister, H. F. Reynolds, conducted rallies and raised support for home and foreign missions. The chief reasons that the Association sought union with other holiness groups was that such might "materially help our missionary work."[22] That was the growing consensus of the Association and of other holiness groups around the country. A connection of holiness churches, possessing compassion for the lost, and a passion to win them to Christ, could do more together than small holiness groups or congregations could do separately. The churches that came together in Chicago in 1907 possessed common impulses toward a practical holiness that reached to the outcasts in urban society, and across the seas to other un-Christianised and needy people. They did not seek to be divisive, but came together, rather, "for the purpose of more securely uniting those who love holiness in the bond of perfect love."[23]

Compromise and Grace for the Sake of Unity

The 1907 union resulted in a balance between the congregational *polity* of the East, where power was centred in the local church, and the more Methodist-like superintendency of the West, where power was centred in the denominational hierarchy. The managerial *episcopacy* of the Methodists had been a primary reason for its surpassing all other denominations in the USA, but it also had restricted holiness preaching. Those in the Association of Pentecostal Churches included former Baptists and Congregationalists were accustomed to local church autonomy. Bresee had modified the Methodist system and allowed local congregations to choose their ministers in consultation with district superintendents, though the denomination held titles to church property. The Association liked keeping property in the hands of local churches but was moving toward greater superintendency for the sake of the supervision of its school, the Pentecostal Collegiate Institute, and for administering home and foreign missions.

The resulting polity balanced superintendency with democratic processes and secured a equalising world church polity in order to fulfil the church's mission. Nazarene polity combined elements of Episcopal, Presbyterian, and Congregational church government. The Nazarene structure, Bresee believed, guaranteed the "liberty of the individual church," and, at the same time, "carefully safeguarded" the "care of the whole church—to maintain such large liberty and yet have arrangements for mobilizing the whole body for efficient work." The superintendency was "limited in its power and yet so efficient in its possibilities, as to minimize dangers and give unity and strength to all parts of the work." [24]The focus was upon whatever would best propagate the holiness message.

Reflecting representative polity, churches elected local church boards as well as delegates to district assemblies. District assemblies elected district boards and their own superintendents as well as delegates to the General Assembly, which elected a General Board that served as the legal corporate board of the church. They also elected "general superintendents," a title congenial to people who had been chastened by "bishops." The church's *Manual*, patterned on the Methodists' *Discipline*, laid out the church government and could be modified by the General Assembly. Changes to the church's Constitution, including the Articles of Faith, also required two-thirds of the districts to approve. There have been and continue to be modifications to the church's Articles of Faith, but only after careful deliberation and the consensus of the church.

The church's general superintendents functioned much like bishops in other churches. Their role, as stated in the current *Manual*, is "to provide apostolic and visionary spiritual leadership by: articulating mission, casting vision, ordaining members of the clergy, propagating theological coherency, and providing jurisdictional and general administrative oversight for the general church." At the time, clergy included elders and deaconesses. Deaconesses were women assisting the church in various compassionate ministries and elders professed a call to preach, had completed a prescribed Course of Study, and served the church as pastors, educators, administrators, and missionaries.[25]

Nazarenes envisioned their mission being to the neglected poor, but many of those who came together from East and West in 1907 in Chicago were middle class. Observers from the rural, southern part of America wondered whether truly holy people could speak with New England accents or dress as nicely as the Nazarenes. The Southerners, made up of mostly poor renters and few landowners, had given up "costly apparel," even wedding rings, in order to simplify their lives and donate more of their meagre earnings to holiness schools and missions. They worshipped in small clapboard buildings. They were committed to do their part, however small, in the evangelisation of the world. Their vision and their commitment were large. Over twenty percent of what they raised for all purposes went to foreign missions. The Holiness Church of Christ sent missionaries to India, Japan, and Mexico. The college church of Texas Holiness University, near Greenville, Texas, which joined the Church of the Nazarene in 1908, a few months before the Pilot Point Assembly, had sent young Harmon Schmelzenbach to South Africa. To the Southerners' surprise, the urban Nazarenes who gathered in Chicago, including those from Los Angeles, Seattle, Boston, and Brooklyn, preached, prayed, shouted and testified to heart holiness as mightily and sincerely as they themselves and possessed the same sense of mission to the world.[26]

A common search for order as well as the need to sustain missions ultimately drew the Southerners, like the Easterners and Westerners, toward union. By the late nineteenth century, in occasional camp meetings and revivals, certain holiness evangelists preached about healing or the Second Coming instead of focusing on sanctification. A few extremists taught that following entire sanctification a believer might find a third blessing that they termed "fire baptism." Some claimed visions. A small number taught that holiness people must abstain not only from alcohol and tobacco, but from tea, coffee, and even marital relations with their wives or husbands. Leaders of the National Holiness Association abhorred and suppressed such radicalism, as did the majority of people who attended the holiness camp meetings and revivals.[27]

These people, whose often-painful exodus from Methodism and other denominations, leaving family and friends behind, made up the early Nazarenes, centred themselves upon holiness. "With great liberty in reference to all things not absolutely essential to holiness," Bresee wrote a few months before the 1907 union with the Association of Pentecostal Churches of America, "the one thing which all agree is the great truth, of the power of the cleansing blood through the baptism with the Holy Ghost. This has saved from division as well as from worldliness and fanaticism." Though early Nazarenes believed in divine healing, they feared that emphasis upon it distracted from the gospel. Though they believed in the Second Coming, they were not dogmatic enough to claim biblical sanction for pre-millennialism or any other particular version of the Second Coming.

Stalwarts in the holiness movement and in the early history of the Church of the Nazarene included not only Methodists, but those from various backgrounds, including Baptists and a few Presbyterians. As well, they came from the Society of Friends and the Salvation Army, neither of which attended to sacraments. Methodists baptised babies, but others did not. Theologies and practises of baptism, long divisive in Protestant history, did not overly concern early Nazarenes. As Bresee said: "A Nazarene might be healed by faith or be sick unto death, a pre- or post-millennialist, and know the power of the blood in the Holy Ghost and shout his triumphant way into the infinite glory of the kingdom of Many Mansions. But the one thing is always prevalent and predominant: 'The blood of Jesus Christ His son cleanseth us from all sin.'"[28]

Just as Wesley had intended of the Methodists, the purpose was to "Christianise Christianity" by being "yeast" or "leaven" within the whole. Nazarenes were to be a church within the Church, with an on-going responsibility to the Church. Methodists in Great Britain, soon after the death of Wesley, had organised themselves like other dissenting bodies outside the Church of England. Now, similarly, holiness people in America sought consolidation in order to sustain the vitality of holiness. Rather than remaining a marginalised group within Methodism, holiness people believed that the best way to propagate holiness within Christianity, and, at the same time, to counteract extremism, was to organise. While the holiness people who became Nazarenes feared ritualism and formalism in worship, they equally feared fanaticism. After the turn of the twentieth century, the threat of Pentecostalism even more hastened holiness people to order themselves in denominations.[29]

Those holiness people who came together in Chicago in 1907 and in Pilot Point in 1908 aimed for the Church of the Nazarene to be a large-canopied church, not a narrow-minded sect—a church able to embrace the widest possible spectrum of persons and places uniting upon one essential. Bresee did not found simply a mission to the neglected poor, though the poor were dear to his heart. Bresee had firm convictions regarding the prohibition of liquor and urged members to vote only for political candidates who would support the suppression of saloons. Bresee did not intend, though, for the church to represent partisan political positions. The Church of the Nazarene was a "believers' church" in the Methodist tradition. That is, those who came out of older denominations wanted a membership made up only of born-again believers. It was not enough to have been born in a Christian home or raised in a good church; to be a Nazarene member one needed to have undergone a clear, personal conversion. Nazarenes were "shouting" Methodists. But they were more than that. That was not reason enough to separate themselves. They were committed to the experience and doctrine of entire sanctification. That was their reason-to-be.[30]

So desirous of the Easterners and Westerners to embrace the Southerners in the galleries of the 1907 Chicago union, that the Assembly added an Article of Faith affirming the Second Coming of Christ, an issue of importance in the mournful South, and a further statement under "Special Advices" affirming Divine Healing. Neither statement was as strong as the Southerners desired. The Second Coming Article of Faith explicitly said that the church did not regard the "numerous theories" regarding the Second Coming as "essential to salvation," and so granted to members "full liberty of belief" regarding this issue. So broad was the church on the Second Coming that a staunch post-millennialist, A. M. Hills, and a resolute a-millennialist, Olive Winchester, could teach for decades alongside convinced pre-millennialists in the church's college religion departments.

The matter of adding rules to the Nazarene *Manual* came to the fore at the 1908 Assembly in Pilot Point. The Holiness Church of Christ had invited the Church of the Nazarene to hold its Assembly there, just a year after the Chicago Assembly, with the hope and anticipation of union. The Holiness Church of Christ itself was the product of the 1904 merger of the New Testament Church of Christ, led by Mary Lee Harris, and the Independent Holiness Church, led chiefly by C. B. Jernigan. To appease Southerners, the assembly voted to add a "special advice" on tobacco, insisting that "those whom we fellowship as members of the Church must be free from this evil, both as to use and sale." That the Southerners wanted a rule against tobacco, a staple crop in Southern states, marked not only their understanding of holiness, but their marginality within tobacco plantation cultures. The Southerners also argued for a statement that members "abstain from membership in, or fellowship with, worldly, secret, or other oath-bound lodges and fraternities." The stand against secret societies aimed primarily against the Freemasons, as not a few prominent Methodists (including American President William McKinley) had joined the Freemasons.

Personally, Bresee believed that such matters, though important, could be left up to inner negotiations between a believer and the ever-convicting Holy Spirit. But for the sake of forging a truly national denomination, he was willing to compromise and insert statements on these issues in the *Manual*. When the Southerners further insisted on a rule prohibiting jewellery, including wedding rings, former Methodist H. D. Brown of Seattle had had enough. Union was not worth the price of legalism. "Mr. Chairman," Brown said, "Let them go." Again, as the debate on rules continued, "Mr. Chairman, let them go." "We cannot let them go," finally said Bresee, who was chairing the Assembly. "They are our own folks." The *Manual* added lines against "indulgence of pride in dress or behaviour," and quietly removed the ring from the matrimony ritual. The vote was unanimous in favour of union. At a time when the North and South still separated the Methodist, Presbyterian, and Baptist denominations, in the Church of the Nazarene North, South, East and West came together.[31]

In many ways, Nazarenes positioned themselves in contrast to the prevailing norms of culture. However, like Americans as a whole, those at the 1908 assembly did not include African Americans. Yet, the year before, at the height of racially discriminating laws in the American South that segregated and subjugated African Americans, the Holiness Association of Texas had passed a resolution on "The Race Problem." "With humiliation we confess that we and our fathers, of the white race, of this country, have not done near as much as we might have done toward the well-being and advancement of the coloured race and are willing to take our part of the blame for the un-neighbourly and unbrotherly feeling which has sprung up and seems to be growing every day." The white race, said the Texas Association, ought to take the initiative in "correcting the wrong, and effecting a reconciliation, and if we have the spirit of Christ, to accomplish this, we will be willing even to yield up some of our rights and preferences, to suffer wrong rather than do wrong." The Texas Association pledged its support to any who might feel a special call to labour among the "coloured" people. Nonetheless, sadly, the Pilot Point union of like-minded holiness people paid more attention to rules than to race. More than eighty years later, Nazarenes of Los Angeles elected Roger Bowman, an African American, as District Superintendent.[32]

The Pilot Point Assembly preceded by more than a decade the debates that tore Presbyterian and Baptist denominations apart into Modernist and Fundamentalist camps. The battles over biblical inerrancy and evolution were not our battles. These were not the issues over which Nazarenes came to be. The *Manual* of the People's Evangelical Church, the mother church in the East, stated, "We believe that the Holy Bible, containing the Scriptures of the Old and New Testaments, is the revelation of divine truth, and the record of God's will, from whence we derive all correct knowledge of religious truth and duty; and that it is the only sufficient rule of a Christian's faith and practice." Similarly, the 1897 Constitution of the Association of Pentecostal Churches of America stated that the Holy Scriptures were "His inspired Word, and the only rule of faith and practice." The Nazarene *Manual* stated simply that the Holy Scriptures are "given by Divine inspiration, revealing the will of God concerning us in all things necessary to our salvation; so that whatever is not contained therein, and cannot be proved thereby, is not to be enjoined as an article of faith." Nazarenes took this statement nearly verbatim from the Church of England. It placed the emphasis upon the Bible's purpose, to show men and women the pathway to salvation.[33]

The Spread and Growth of the Nazarene Denomination

Holiness people believed that a sanctified life was marked by love and that love compelled service. In the rural South, the Holiness Church of Christ maintained so-called "rescue cottages." In these homes, pregnant women gave birth to their babies away from prying eyes and gossiping mouths, and, if they chose, could leave their babies in the hands of caring workers who would find homes for them among Christian families.[34]

As decades went by, revivals and camp meetings remained a large part of the church around the world as well as in North America. Those who inherited the church from their parents feared decline from the purposes and practises of the founders and longed to remain true to their parents' godly heritage. Not unlike the second generation of similar movements, Nazarenes wondered how they might keep the "glory down." In addition to efficient management, the second generation tried to keep "the tempo up."[35] They preached and sang loud and long, repeated holiness terminology, and tightened rules. During the Great Depression, Nazarenes sacrificed in many ways in order to keep the Nazarene schools open and missionaries on the field. They sold jewellery and property. They prayed and fasted. Per capita, Nazarenes gave more than members of other, larger denominations. In membership, during the 1930s the Church of the Nazarene was the fastest growing denomination in America.

When General Superintendents Roy T. Williams, John Goodwin, and James B. Chapman delivered their quadrennial address to the 1940 General Assembly, after a decade of remarkable church growth, they described the Church of the Nazarene as "a religion that combines head and heart, reason and emotion." The General Superintendents worried that the church might lower its standards. "To fail here," they said, "is to endanger the doctrine, the government, the policies, the objectives, and the ethical standards for which we have been a called-out people." At the same time, the General Superintendents warned that legalism, which they defined as "law without love," would draw the church away from grace. They saw in the future the dangers of professionalism, which was substituting creeds and programs for the presence and power of the Holy Spirit.[36]

During the Second World War, missions' director C. W. Jones had been standing poised and waiting for peace before sending out a backlog of waiting, eager, new missionary recruits. The church amassed financial resources for expansion. Giving to the foreign missions' program of the church more than doubled during the war, reaching well over a half-million dollars by 1944. J. B. Chapman issued a call for even greater giving and mobilisation. The possibilities of entering new fields excited church leaders and laypeople. The number of missionaries stood at 78 in 1944, but surpassed 200 by 1948, 300 by the close of the next quadrennium in 1952, and over 400 by 1960. By 1976 there were 550 Nazarene missionaries. Prosperity meant that Nazarenes did not need to live quite so simply in order to finance their colleges and missions program. With others, they moved from farms and inner cities to the suburbs.[37]

Another generation, coming of age during the social turmoil of the 1960s and 1970s, called back to collective memory John Wesley as both theologian and social reformer. The writings and spirit of John Wesley became a means of redefining and repositioning the church. Recalling the nineteenth century holiness movement as well as Bresee's passion for the urban poor, when calamities hit Guatemala in 1976, Nazarenes began major works of compassion. That was a new beginning to the church's localised response to devastation, hunger, and poverty. Turning to their own urban past history and preference for the poor, Nazarenes also began to seek regeneration in blighted cities. They reached out to ethnic minorities and welcomed emigrants from their own mission fields. Haitian Creole and Spanish-speaking congregations began. Nazarenes found fair processes of internationalisation of the church that would allow any Nazarene from around the world full representation. These evidences of practical divinity did not alter the high value the church placed on organisation, or the temptation of local Nazarenes, now rid of embarrassingly identifying traits of dress and behaviour and encumbering rules, to accommodate to culture, and to attach themselves to prevailing social and political winds. Although institutionalism loomed over the church, God's Spirit loomed larger than this, and broke through in new ways and with new words amid structure. That is Nazarene faith, that God can sanctify and use humanity, meaning not only individuals but structures, even churchly ones. The Nazarene historian Mendell Taylor said many years ago that whenever denominational structures block or thwart the Spirit's moving, which is like a mighty river, God forges another channel. God keeps raising up people among whom he is able to pour out his Spirit.[38] Bresee himself said, "If the channels are kept open God's grace will continue to flow through us to [women and] men."[39]

Will we remain a people among whom God is pouring out his Spirit? A people listening to his voice, compliant to his will?[40] We are walking alongside and talking with Christ, who reveals to us more and more of himself, and directs our pathways to our destination. We are not just two, but more than two and a half million. We can be a people listening to and responding creatively to the movement of God's Spirit. We are still in the process of becoming what we are intended to be. We have not arrived. We are a people still on a journey, a people with a mission.

DISCUSSION QUESTIONS

1. What was the purpose upon which the Church of the Nazarene was formed? In what ways is your local congregation still aligned with this purpose?

2. What are your thoughts on the idea of "Christianising Christianity" as a basis for reaching unbelievers? How would this look in today's world and in your local church?

3. What were some of the things that distinguished the Church of the Nazarene from other denominations? Do you still think these distinctions are present? Do you still think these distinctions are necessary?

4. Does your local church have a heart for and an emphasis on the poor and marginalised? Is this an important emphasis for Nazarenes? Why or why not?

5. What are some of the compromises that were made for union that surprised you? Do any of these same issues still cause division in your local church? What can we learn for Bresee and others about compromise and unity in the midst of differences?

6. What is the Church of the Nazarene's system of government? Please consult the *Church of the Nazarene Manual 2017-2021* (http://nazarene.org/organization/general-secretary/manual). What parts are difficult to understand?

CHAPTER 3

HOLINESS IN THOUGHT, WORD, AND DEED

For more than one hundred years, as Nazarenes have walked with Christ, our desire has not been primarily to transmit doctrine. Rather, we are consumed with a right relationship with God in Christ through his Spirit. To possess and pass on doctrines that are not experienced is called scholasticism. Yet, at the same time, doctrine provides the intellectual structure through which the Spirit works. The call to holiness itself has compelled plain communication in every generation and culture.

Wesley and the Message of Holiness

Nazarenes believe that the holiness message penetrates the Bible and flows throughout the Church's history. Contemplative monks such as Bernard of Clairvaux and Catholic mystics like Teresa of Avila drew upon the traditions of Greek Fathers such as Irenaeus and Gregory of Nyssa. Likewise, Wesley's understanding of sanctification was influenced by the Greek Fathers (as well as the Latin Fathers) to the extent that it could be said that he spoke sanctification with a Greek accent. The Wesleyan heritage, in turn, provided the Church of the Nazarene with a British accent, especially as the hymns of Charles Wesley (John's brother) penetrated into the life of the movement. "And Can it Be," for instance, pled: "Died he for me, who caused his pain, for me, who him to death pursued?" "Amazing love! How can it be that Thou, my God, should die for me?" Another verse went, "Long my imprisoned spirit lay, fast bound in sin and nature's night." Then God "diffused a quick'ning ray," and I, the sinner, "woke," and the "dungeon flamed with light!" "Chains fell off"—and I rose and went forth to follow Christ. Hymns held the Methodist movement together in both thought and spirit. Scripture filled the lines. The hymns were prayers for holiness. Hymns brought theology to the people. The Wesleys' *Collection of Hymns for the Use of the People Called Methodists*, published in 1780, provided, in John Wesley's estimation, a "distinct and full ... account of Scriptural Christianity."[41]

The Church of the Nazarene considered itself John Wesley's "legitimate and historic offspring," as B. F. Haynes, the first editor of the *Herald of Holiness*, wrote. "In point of doctrine, of experience, of evangelistic activity and missionary belief and endeavor," the Church of the Nazarene is the "direct successor of the Wesleyan movement. There is not a single truth in which we believe that was not stressed by Mr. Wesley."[42] Bresee agreed that it was the calling of the Church of the Nazarene to revitalise the doctrines of Wesley, not to create any new. "The Church of the Nazarene did not have its origin so much in an effort to establish a doctrinal truth," said Bresee, "as in the experience of truth already recognized."

Following Wesley, Nazarenes desired to recover the New Testament's message of holiness without rejecting the teachings of the Church in the intervening centuries. The church's beliefs, Bresee explained, were "the common orthodox doctrines of the church."[43] Nazarenes learned from the theological conclusions of the early church councils as embedded in the Articles of Religion of the Church of England and the Methodist Church. The language of the Nicene Creed penetrated the Church of the Nazarene's statements on the Triune God, for instance. The church affirmed "one eternally existent, infinite God, Sovereign of the universe; that He only is God, creative and administrative, holy in nature, attributes, and purpose; that He, as God, is Triune in essential being, revealed as Father, Son, and Holy Spirit." Likewise, the Church of the Nazarene attested that Jesus Christ "was one with the Father; that He became incarnate by the Holy Spirit and was born of the Virgin Mary, so that two whole and perfect natures, that is to say the Godhead and manhood, are thus united in one Person very God and very man, the God-man."

The Holiness Movement's Influence on Nazarene Theology

Holiness revivalism contextualised Wesley's message for nineteenth century North America and washed back over into the British Isles. The work of reinterpreting the holiness message rested on the heart of Methodist theologian Phoebe Palmer. She held "Tuesday Afternoon Meetings for the Promotion of Holiness" in her New York City home. Palmer linked the baptism with the Holy Spirit to the moment of entire sanctification. Pentecost brought to the disciples both purity and power to boldly witness. If believers fully consecrated themselves, doing their part, God would respond, doing his part and sanctify through and through. She told those who exercised faith for entire sanctification to believe the biblical promises. One of the promises, based on Exodus 29:37 and Matthew 23:19, was that the altar sanctified the gift. This was more than a metaphor. Revivalists encouraged believers to bow at kneeling rails, to receive there and then sanctifying grace. Palmer's "shorter way" to holiness fit the utilitarian and pragmatic character of the American mindset. Whereas Wesley told those of his followers who thought they might be entirely sanctified to wait until there was both inner assurance and fruits of the Spirit, Palmer encouraged individuals to testify boldly to the second blessing.[44]

Another departure related to the holiness movement's interpretation of the Israelites' pilgrimage from Egypt to the Promised Land. Holiness evangelists saw the new birth of believers as analogous to the liberation of the Israelites from bondage in Egypt; it was their liberation from sin. The forty years wandering in the wilderness corresponded to Christian life following the new birth, filled with disappointment, disobedience, and defeat. The crossing over Jordan into Canaan symbolised the victory that awaited believers upon their entire sanctification. This departed from other Christian analogies in which one's "crossing over into Jordan" was death.

The appeal of holiness related to a sense of the present outpouring of the Holy Spirit—not only upon individuals but also society. Charles Finney, a Congregationalist revivalist, in particular, worked to eradicate slavery and as President of Oberlin College to educate women and African Americans. Finney emphasised consistent devotion to the will of God. "Entire" sanctification was, to him, the continued dependency of the believer upon God. Finney's reading of Wesley and Methodist theologians as well as his own study convinced him that the baptism with the Holy Spirit followed the new birth and that Pentecost fulfilled the Old Testament promise of the Holy Spirit.[45]

Nazarene worship was the product of revivalism. There were not many rituals or liturgies. Instead, there were lively and singable hymns and songs that conveyed the message of holiness. Methodist Fanny Crosby wrote "Rescue the Perishing" in 1869 after visiting a New York City inner-city mission. The plea of the hymn was not to judge or condemn, but to reach out in pity, to "weep over the erring one." Sensing the tenderness, children and young people joined adults in worship. The testimonies, music, and sermon illustrations appealed to children. All of these pointed hearers toward submission to the Word.[46]

While many of Wesley's hymns were prayers for holiness, the holiness movement boldly affirmed the present attainment of sanctifying grace. "Holiness unto the Lord," written in 1900 by Methodist Lelia Morris, became the unofficial banner or "watchword and song" of the Church of the Nazarene. God calls the church out of the world. God enables his people to be "children of light" and to walk with Jesus in "garments of white," without being sullied or contaminated while all around was darkness and sin. The emphasis was Wesleyan: that holiness was "not our own righteousness," but "Christ within"—living, reigning, and saving from sin.

The revival tradition stressed the decisive moments of both conversion and entire sanctification. The most hardened sinner might enter a revival meeting and hear the gospel, might find the courage to come forward during the "altar call," might kneel there ardently repenting, and might immediately find Christ's forgiveness, rest, and peace.

As well as a means of making Christians of adults, conversion was a rite of initiation for the children and adolescents of the church. They saw their parents' lives, participated in family devotions, attended Sunday School, read the Bible as best they could, listened to testimonies, witnessed altar calls, and responded to the Word. In a "believer's church," children and adolescents needed to personally repent and seek the forgiveness of Christ. Similarly, those who had been "saved" looked for remaining sin. Preachers described the sin as "Adamic," original sin, consisting of carnality, pride of self, idolatry, and self-centeredness. This remaining sin could be cleansed by a "second work of grace," and that was the expectation of those who grew up in the church.

This sort of narrative ran through the testimonies of thousands. One oft-told story was of Reuben "Bud" Robinson, a vice-riddled, illiterate, stuttering cowboy when he stumbled into a revival at age twenty and was saved. From there, he had a call to preach. Reluctantly granted a license to preach by the Methodists, Robinson proceeded to bring hundreds to Christ. As he preached with holiness revivalists, he heard and reheard the message of holiness, he sought entire sanctification, for ten years. Finally, in a cornfield, after an altercation with a stubborn mule, he was sanctified. "Anger boiled up, and God skimmed it off, and pride boiled up, and God skimmed it off, and envy boiled up and God skimmed it off, until it seemed to me that my heart was perfectly empty. I said, 'Lord there won't be anything left of me.' God seemed to say, 'there will not be much left, but what little there is will be clean.'"[47] Robinson's ministry became even more effective. Another early Nazarene, James Chapman, testified that on a certain evening in September 1899, when he was 15 years old, he became convinced that Christ "did forgive my sins and make me his child," and "that on the very next evening he sanctified me wholly."[48]

The influence of holiness revivalism upon the Church of the Nazarene came through many channels. A. M. Hills, a Congregationalist, joined the church in 1912. As a young man, Hills sat under the teaching of Finney. After graduating from Oberlin, Hills went to Yale Divinity School, where he studied under professors shaking off remnants of Calvinism. Afterward, Hills pastored churches in Ohio and Pennsylvania, and then entered evangelism. In 1895, he professed entire sanctification, and quickly rose to prominence among holiness evangelists. His *Holiness and Power* (1897) collected historical and contemporary accounts. Hills became founding president of Texas Holiness University, and served other schools as administrator and teacher, including the Star Hall Mission in Manchester, England. Later, he taught at Pasadena College. His two-volume *Fundamental Christian Theology* (1931), compiled of earlier writings, is filled with diatribes against Calvinism.[49]

Hills defended infant baptism, post-millennialism, and free will as a natural ability of fallen humanity. The latter point, as Hills knew, differed from Wesley. For Wesley, when Adam fell humanity lost its ability to choose what was good; free will was a universal benefit of the atonement. Grace allowed human beings to choose good. Nazarenes taught:

> Since the sin and fall of Adam, all are without spiritual life, and by natural impulse and disposition are averse to God and holiness and inclined to sin. It is not possible that any should turn and prepare themselves by their own natural ability, to faith and calling upon God, or the doing of good works, acceptable and pleasing to Him, without the enabling Spirit and grace of God, which are freely proffered to all men through our Lord Jesus Christ.[50]

Hills thought this statement was too close to the Calvinism that his professors at both Oberlin and Yale had taught him to reject. By the late nineteenth century, Methodist theologians also had departed from Wesley on this very point and taught free will apart from free grace. Hills's *Fundamental Christian Theology* was on the Nazarene Course of Study for only two quadrennia, 1932-1940, but his teachings had a long-lasting influence.[51]

The Nature of Nazarene Theology

The 1919 General Assembly commissioned H. Orton Wiley to write the church's official systematic theology. The first of three volumes appeared in 1940. During the twenty years that Wiley took to write *Christian Theology* he served for ten years as president of Northwest Nazarene College, and then as president (for the second time) of Pasadena College. Wiley, a young protégé of Bresee, undertook his theological education at the Pacific School of Theology and read Methodist theologians, particularly John Miley.

As Wiley was writing, in approaching any particular doctrine, he first delved into the Scriptures. Then he described the doctrine's development in the church. This led him to ancient writers, whom he read in the original Greek or Latin, and medieval and reformed theologians. Wiley kept the Church of the Nazarene loyal to the classic positions of Christian faith. The cardinal doctrine of justification by faith placed Nazarenes squarely with other Protestants. At the same time, Wiley spared the church from Fundamentalism by not identifying its teaching with pre-millennialism and by insisting that the Bible's authority rested in that for which God intended it. For example, Wiley maintained that the "creation hymn" of Genesis answered *who* God was, not how or when he created the universe.[52] Another marker signifying the Nazarene church's distance from Fundamentalism was in its unwavering support for a woman's privilege to be engaged in all ministries and to be ordained.

Hymns popularised Nazarene theology. Haldor Lillenas was to Nazarene hymnody what Charles Wesley was to Methodism. "Glorious Freedom," by Lillenas, revived Charles Wesley's image of being chained in a dungeon, "fast bound in sin and nature's night." Only the Great Emancipator could break the "fetters of sin" and end the struggle with sin—envy, hatred and strife, vain and worldly ambitions and, in short, all that saddened life. Christ brought freedom from pride and love of gold, from evil temper and anger. Lillenas's most widely known song outside the Church of the Nazarene is "Wonderful Grace of Jesus," written in 1918. Through the "transforming power" of grace even the most defiled are made to be "God's dear child." Grace is greater than our sins.

For a century, around the world Nazarene hymns promoted a sense of denominational ethos and loyalty. Honorato T. Reza translated Lillenas's songs, as well as the hymns of Charles Wesley and the holiness revival, into Spanish. In 1962 the Church of the Nazarene published *Gracia y Devocion: Himnario para el Uso De Las Iglesias Evangelicas*. Like the Methodists, because Nazarenes sang their theology, it penetrated their minds and hearts.

Nazarenes moved beyond "holiness triumphalism," which suggested all problems were spiritual and could be solved by either justification or sanctification. Nazarene Theological Seminary Professor Louis A. Reed admitted in 1947, "It is very possible that a person can be a good Christian and yet have mental disorders."[53] Those "saved and sanctified" should not expect to be in perpetual states of joy and happiness. Lewis Corlett in 1952, the same year he became president of Nazarene Theological Seminary, commented that physiological and psychological infirmities and modern society itself, not remaining sin, produced depression. His own brother, D. Shelby Corlett, had had to resign in 1948 from his 12-year editorship of the *Herald of Holiness*, due to depression. The reason for depression, Lewis Corlett wrote, "lies in the physical and mental rather than in the spiritual."[54]

Humanness must be distinguished from carnality, said J. Kenneth Grider. Peter was still prejudiced against Gentiles and had much to learn even after Pentecost, Grider noted. Though no one would be born with racial prejudice, it could certainly be a part of one's upbringing and thus become an involuntary part of one's thinking and behaving. Normally, Nazarenes had considered "temper and anger" to be the result of evil. Grider said that it may be from carnality, but it also may be the result of one's personality or upbringing. Some might be naturally prone to quick emotions. This was no excuse for not coming to greater control in this area of their lives; one must grow in grace. Nonetheless, the point brought great relief to Nazarenes for whom losing one's temper was a problem remaining after many trips to a kneeling rail. As a result, Nazarene preaching in the 1970s and onward became less crisis-oriented and more need-focused. Not every sermon need end in an altar call; not every spiritual, much less psychological, problem was solvable that way. Nazarene laypersons, including pastors and their spouses, became more open about depression and other emotional difficulties.[55]

The Revival of John Wesley in the Church of the Nazarene

This appraisal of what sanctification might or might not accomplish in a person's life related to the church's rediscovery of John Wesley. In addition to his understanding of free grace, Wesley added the dimension of prevenient grace—the grace that "goes before" all human beings as a universal benefit of the atonement to lead them to Christ. Wesley provided a needed corrective to the under-emphases of the holiness movement upon the processes of Christian formation and growth in grace. Wesley's *A Plain Account of Christian Perfection* showed that holiness was not absolute, or infallible. Nor did it mean freedom from temptations or infirmities. Christian perfection was always "improvable" and centred in love.

Wesley would not have been surprised that Wiley and others found broader theological streams than just those of the nineteenth-century holiness movement, or even Wesley himself. Wesley believed his teachings to be thoroughly biblical and based upon centuries of Church teaching.[56]

Mildred Bangs Wynkoop was among the Nazarene theologians influenced by a rediscovery of Wesley. Her parents had helped start the Church of the Nazarene in Seattle, and as a young girl she remembered hearing Bresee preach. Wynkoop studied under Wiley at both Northwest Nazarene College and Pasadena College, helping him with early drafts of his *Christian Theology*. She began graduate education in her forties, and in 1955 earned a doctorate in theology. She and her husband, Ralph Wynkoop, pastored and travelled as evangelists, and from 1960 to 1966 the Wynkoops served in Taiwan and in Japan. In Japan, Wynkoop realised how difficult it was for Japanese to conceive of sin; for them, right relationships structured society. Wynkoop emphasised that original sin represented a distorted relationship with God, not a "thing" to be uprooted. She feared that a "credibility gap" existed between what Nazarenes professed and how they lived, and this came, in part, from placing the "circumstance" or "crisis" of holiness above its "content," which was love, and "goal," which was Christ-likeness. Wynkoop said that one maintained a right relationship with God and others by living faithfully from moment to moment in the presence of the Holy Spirit. Wynkoop taught her students to look beyond the first two verses of Romans 12 to see the whole chapter as defining holiness lived within community. Wynkoop's *A Theology of Love* (1972) represented a significant shift in holiness theology.[57]

Embodied Social Holiness

From Wesley and Wynkoop, a stream of holiness theology emphasised the social and collective nature of holiness. Wesley advocated obedience to state and church, and still offered what would be called a preferential option for the poor. Wesley said: "Let justice, mercy and truth govern all our minds and actions. Let our superfluities give way to our neighbour's conveniences...our conveniences to our neighbour's necessities; our necessities to his [or her] extremities."[58] Love for God changed human beings' values and ways of life. The Sermon on the Mount (Matthew 5–7) provided an ethic for this time and this place. Wesley described both personal and systemic sin, both personal and social redemption.[59]

In the third and fourth generations of a movement, the retrieval of a forgotten past justifies a new direction into the future. The generation coming of age during the social turmoil of the 1960s and 1970s called back to collective memory of Wesley and nineteenth century social movements. Timothy Smith reminded a generation of Nazarenes that "the nineteenth-century quest for holiness was turned into avenues of service, instead of the byways of mystic contemplation."[60] Smith commented: "Evidence has multiplied that holiness preaching was from Francis Asbury and time onward an important catalyst to Methodist participation in American movement for social justice."[61] Both the Wesleyan Church and the Free Methodist Church separated from the Methodist Episcopal Church over its tolerance of slave-holding members. The pursuit of holiness accompanied anti-slavery campaigns, movements to grant preaching as well as voting rights to women, and, because it was a social issue, the prohibition of alcohol. As well, it was recalled, holiness people built orphanages and homes for unwed mothers, and conducted storefront rescue missions for the homeless and poor. In Nazarene history itself, the church had a long record of social concern. In China, the Nazarene work included Bresee Memorial Hospital and projects such as distributing relief from the Red Cross in a time of famine, helping to build a dam to prevent the Yellow River, which flowed through the Nazarene field, from flooding, overseeing the construction of an asphalt road from Handan to Daming, and initiating brick-making and basket-weaving industries. The church provided a system of primary schools for girls as well as boys. One missionary taught old women how to read.

While such ministries characterised mission fields, in the USA the unity of personal and social ethics broke down in the 1920s, during the Fundamentalist-Modernist controversy. The holiness denominations emphasised personal sanctification and the Methodists social transformation. On the forefront of the social gospel movement and ecumenism, Methodists stressed the organisational genius of their founder, and his emphasis on religious experience—but not his theology. They quoted (out of context from a sermon that had a lot to say about the importance of Christian orthodoxy) Wesley's statement, "if your heart is right, give me your hand." Holiness groups, meanwhile, retreated. They did not covet influence in society.[62]

Eventually, however, Nazarenes realised that Christ-like love necessitated involvement and sought the reintegration of personal holiness with social commitment. Home Missions Director Raymond Hurn wrote that the church must not crawl into its "own little enclave, polish the saints, refuse contact with outsiders, maintain personal piety, and totally miss the real mission of Christ in the world."[63]

Wynkoop's *John Wesley: Christian Revolutionary* (1970), fit a time when protests and violence tore apart many societies. In America, the origins of social disruption were racial and economic as well as generational. Wynkoop reminded Nazarenes that "the very thing which our [holiness] forefathers had, essentially, was the spirit of revolution. They were not quiet, comfortable, placid, undisturbed people. They seethed with energy. They saw visions which sent them crashing through barriers of impossibilities. They dreamed dreams and brought forth sold realities." Wynkoop described Wesleyanism as "sanctified revolution." "This is a young person's religion," she exclaimed. "There is life in it."[64]

Sanctified revolution took the form of compassion. By the 1970s, compassion became a more organised element in the Church of the

Nazarene, as well as other evangelical churches. One catalyst for denominational action was an earthquake that shook Guatemala in 1975, where the Nazarenes had a strong work. A Guatemala Earthquake Reconstruction Fund received $300,000 USD. At the same time, in Haiti, the church undertook a widespread feeding program to go along with its primary schools and literacy programs. The political situation in Nicaragua tore Nazarene families apart, but, during the time of political reconciliation, the Church of the Nazarene joined other Protestants in various rehabilitation movements.[65]

Beyond these responses to devastation, hunger, and poverty, Nazarenes reached out to ethnic minorities in blighted cities such as New York, Washington, DC, San Francisco, Indianapolis, and Dallas, and welcomed immigrants from such countries as Vietnam and Cambodia as well as their own mission fields. Haitian Creole and Spanish-speaking congregations flourished in American cities.[66]

Compassion itself could be structured. In 1984 the Church of the Nazarene established an Office of Compassionate Ministries. In November 1985 the church held an international Conference on Compassionate Ministry at Nazarene Theological Seminary in Kansas City. Those who attended sang Fanny Crosby's "Rescue the Perishing, Care for the Dying" with renewed meaning. For many, there was a close connection among evangelism, compassion, and holiness.[67]

By the twenty-first century, Nazarenes, influenced by a post-denominational and global generation, embraced contemporary praise and worship styles. Guitars, drums, and keyboards replaced organs and pianos. The purpose of songs changed from that of theological affirmation and denominational enculturation to happy adoration. Nazarenes sang the same songs sung in other churches. As they adapted to the cultural contexts of the worshippers, worship retained missional intent, to reach the lost.

The church grew theologically as well. In the twenty-first century, theologians in Latin America, Africa, and Asia posed new questions, such as the relationship between the Spirit and the spirit world, and the relationship between holiness and poverty and oppression. A longing for a truly biblical theology and authentically biblical preaching accompanied the broadening appropriation of tradition, which, in turn, led back to the Trinity. The Triune nature of God signified the relational nature of God himself. Global theology conferences held in Guatemala (2002), the Netherlands (2007), South Africa (2014), and the USA (2018) demonstrated the centrality of compassion and justice to the church's understanding of holiness, as did a major conference on Compassionate Ministries at Olivet Nazarene University in 2017. In each of these gatherings, global theologians and leaders taught that holiness could not be a solitary pursuit. When God redeemed, God did so within community and through community, and set believers in his Church. Long-term Nazarene missionary to Papua New Guinea and Fiji, Neville Bartle, observed: "Because of the intense individualism of Western society, holiness has often been thought of as internal, personal, and to a large extent, private. The concept of separation from the world has also encouraged isolated personal holiness." This model does not fit the Bible. Bartle commented: "Instead of thinking about the implications of being a 'child of God,' we need to think more about the social implications of being the 'people of God' in a more collective sense."[68] Believers were to embody a community-based holiness and work together for justice and social transformation.

Conclusion

Nazarene theology centres upon Christian holiness. This is its legacy. Nazarenes ask their most learned theologians to speak plainly to God's people, show the implications, and map it out. Nazarenes are not content with propositional papers and declarations. We have the knowledge; what then must we *do*?

While Nazarenes were walking along conversing with Christ, they seemed to hear: "It is good to believe rightly, but as we go on a little farther, do not miss *doing* what is essential here and now." And as they walked further: "In the past you have been obsessed with lesser things while I was imprisoned, naked, and hungry."

The twenty-first century church possessed more humility. There was more seeking and a less "we have found it" mentality. This greater restraint fit a questing generation. Not only that, it fit the best of Wesleyan tradition.

DISCUSSION QUESTIONS

1. What was the place of hymns in the history of the Wesleyan and Holiness movements and how has this changed today? How is Wesleyan-Holiness theology being taught in your church? What theology is being taught by some of the songs used in your local church?

2. What are some of the different ways that the Church of the Nazarene has pursued holiness? What are the positives and negatives about these different ways?

3. What are some ways that your local church has and is pursuing holiness?

4. Is there a danger of legalism or fundamentalism in the way we pursue holiness? What are you doing to assure this doesn't happen personally and in your local church?

5. What is your understanding of the social dimension of holiness?

6. What are the connections between holiness, evangelism, and compassion? What happens when we stress one of these too much and ignore the others?

CHAPTER 4

LEADERSHIP AND MISSION IN THE CHURCH OF THE NAZARENE

In order to accomplish the Great Commission, the Church of the Nazarene formed a tight, centralised, international structure with well-articulated lines of responsibility. The mission—based on Jesus's preaching, teaching, and healing—balanced evangelism, education, and compassionate ministries. All three were evident from the beginning.

Organisation for Mission

"The Church needs an order of knighthood that shall as thoroughly renounce the world as did ever Ignatius or St. Francis," said Bresee. He aspired to see a group of men and women who were "in the world but not of it," who were "utterly without love for its wealth or honor or place" in order to bear the message of divine love.[69] Nazarene missionaries were something like the local preachers Wesley commissioned in his day, and the circuit riders that Asbury sent up and down the Atlantic seaboard and across the Appalachian Mountains. Like Wesley and Asbury, Nazarene mission leaders, Reynolds and his successors, knew where the needs of the church were. Not local churches, but the church as a whole was responsible for choosing, equipping, and sending missionaries.

Nazarenes built an international church based on districts, not national churches. Outside of North America, because of language differences as well as geographic distances, missionary superintendents acted in the stead of general superintendents. There developed a "regional" system, attempted from 1926 to 1928 and then re-implemented in 1976, in which general leaders appointed regional and field directors. This particular arrangement replicated the Methodist managerial episcopacy more than the democratic system but served well the administrative needs of the rapidly growing church.

The early establishment of a unified and general budget allowed the church to expand strategically. Impressive for the size of the denomination is the number of missionaries that the church sent, schools that the church established, and money that the church spent to support its global enterprise. In 2017 the Church of the Nazarene sent out 700 missionaries from 50 world areas; its membership reached 2.55 million with 30,875 congregations in 162 countries. Currently, Seventy-five percent of Nazarenes live outside the United States and Canada. Thirty percent are in Africa, and another thirty percent in Central and South America and the Caribbean. Nazarene men and women in remote corners of the world belong (and know they belong) to something far beyond themselves, something global.

The 2017-2021 Board of General Superintendents included Eugenio Duarte, born in Cape Verde, who had served as Africa Region Director before being elected a General in 2009. Duarte was the first African to serve as General Superintendent. David Graves, also elected in 2009, had been a pastor and director of Sunday School Ministries. Gustavo Crocker, born in Guatemala, was elected in 2013 while serving as Eurasia Region Director. David Busic, also elected in 2013, was then serving as president of Nazarene Theological Seminary. In 2017, the General Assembly elected Filimao Chambo, born in Mozambique, who was Africa Regional Director, and Carla Sunberg, who had been raised in Germany, had been a missionary to Russia, and who then was serving as president of Nazarene Theological Seminary. Sunberg is the second woman to serve as a general superintendent, following in the footsteps of Nina Gunter, who served from 2005 to 2009.

The General Board is representational, dependent upon the number of church members on the region. The 2017-2021 General Board consisted of 53 members: 48 regional members, plus five members, two representing educational institutions, and one each representing Nazarene Missions, Nazarene Youth, and Sunday School and Discipleship Ministries. A more-or-less equal number of ministers and laypersons make up the General Board. Twenty-eight of the regional members represent areas outside of the USA and Canada.

The Influence of Hiram F. Reynolds

Reynolds more than Bresee shaped the organisational patterns of the church. Reynolds, as General Superintendent from 1907 to 1932, and as Secretary of Foreign Missions from 1908 to 1922, and again from 1925 to 1927, expected respect for the authority and fretted whenever missionaries became too independent. He emphasised evangelism and therein the cardinal doctrine of the church, justification. Leaders passed on to pastors, missionaries, educators, and laypersons this emphasis upon superintendency in order to accomplish the mission. For Reynolds, there was room for cooperation with other denominations in order to accomplish the Great Commission. The Church of the Nazarene in India ministered within certain defined boundaries in rural Maharashtra, and the same obedience to partnership arrangements held true in China, Peru, Swaziland, and other countries.[70]

Reynolds's directorship of missions began in the Association of Pentecostal Churches of America. Hastily, as the first missionaries were embarking for Bombay, Reynolds and other members of the missions committee drafted a policy for India. Reynolds required M. D. Wood, the pioneer missionary, to wait for approval before making major decisions, a long wait since in that day it took several months to get messages back and forth across the Atlantic and Indian Oceans. The church would *not* be made up of self-governing national churches, but, rather, an international body subject to centralised governance.

Reynolds, whose time preceded later missiologists' reflections on contextualisation, believed that there would be common manifestations of holiness—how it would be preached, taught, and lived—irrespective of the society. Under Reynolds's preaching in mission fields such as Japan, sinners were saved and gave up their vices and believers came into the "second blessing." Revival methods were effective everywhere.

Revival came to the Nazarene field in China in 1927 with the repentant spirit of missionary Aaron J. Smith toward a lowly worker on the compound in Daming. Missionaries prayed and fasted during noontime; students from the Bible school asked that they might too. Missionaries rejoiced when Chinese converts prayed, shouted hallelujah and amen, and confessed their sins in ways that missionaries, labouring under their own worldviews, could identify as a genuine movement of the sanctifying Spirit. "When the Holy Ghost gets hold of a man," said Smith, "I care not of what nation or tribe or language he may be, there will be the same manifestation of the Holy Spirit which has been peculiar to all the holy people of all ages."[71] L. C. Osborn, another missionary, realised that he had been mistaken as to how the Chinese would react once they "got through."[72] Soon the students began to spread the revival to their home churches and villages. Many, including missionaries themselves, became convinced that missionaries were unneeded.[73]

Successive policies maintained that the "work and manifestations of the Holy Spirit are practically the same in all countries." The church lost a degree of freedom to make the message culturally meaningful, but propagated the experience, the doctrines, and the language of holiness over which it had come to exist.[74]

Under Reynolds, Nazarene missionaries embraced the "three-selfs" goals of self-propagation, self-support, and self-government. These accorded well with Anglo-American virtues of independency, hard work, and self-determination. When mission fields reached the three-selfs goals, local districts would stand on their own. Self-support was measurable, but with expanding districts, schools, hospitals, and literature development, difficult to achieve. Reynolds envisioned an international church made up of self-supporting districts that one day would need no missionary supervision, with equal rights, privileges, and responsibilities. In regard to self-government, due to the centralised nature of Nazarene polity, the commitment of the church toward developing fully self-governing bodies, was different. Unlike Baptists and other congregational denominations and faith missions, the Church of the Nazarene tied its churches tightly together. Internationalisation promised members from around the world full representation.

Those who followed Reynolds's thought linked entire sanctification to Pentecost and the power that Pentecost gave to the disciples to evangelise. The Holy Spirit gave power both to cast out demons and to translate the gospel into many languages, and bestowed on believers the ability to witness boldly, said theologian J. Glenn Gould in 1935. "The Nazarene work is an evangelistic movement," Gould wrote, "our genius lies along this line. To this end were we called forth." Nazarenes, he warned, must avoid allowing church buildings, schools, colleges, hospitals, or orphanages, at home or abroad, to become ends in themselves. Gould devised his thoughts within an evangelical subculture growing uneasy with anything that seemed like a "social" gospel.[75]

Both education and compassionate ministries served evangelistic ends. "Our policy is not primarily one of education," wrote C. Warren Jones in 1955, "but the salvation of the heathen," and evangelism "must always stand above education in importance." Though the church believed in "social uplift," Jones cautioned, these goals "must come second to preaching for personal Christian experience." In regard to health programs, said Jones, "we are for medical missions, but only as a means to an end, and that end must be the salvation of the lost."[76] Missionary Bronell Greer, who went to India in 1944 and served there for 46 years, complained that educational and medical institutions were strangling evangelism and perpetuating dependency. The Great Commission of the church was not to heal the sick or to reform society, he protested, but to preach the gospel. "All divinely ordained work of the church has its importance," Greer agreed, "but not all God given vocations are equally important. Evangelism holds the highest priority."[77]

The Influence of Phineas Bresee

For Bresee, educational, medical, and other compassionate ministries need not be justified on the basis of their contribution to evangelism. Deeds of love flowed naturally out of sanctified hearts. For him, Christians would act compassionately because perfect love filled their hearts; it is simply part of their following Christ. If any act, no matter how noble, were only a means toward an end, it could not be said to be pure. Tending to the disadvantaged was a manifestation of holiness, the mission for which the Church of the Nazarene came to be. The church's very name embraced the idea of being among those looked down upon. "Nothing good," Jews thought, comes out of Nazareth (John 1:46). With derision Paul was called the "ringleader of the Nazarene sect" (Acts 24:4).Nazarenes would go to the despised, regardless of race, ethnicity, or class and embrace them with the love of Jesus Christ.

What kind of gospel would it be that hoarded resources and failed to give compassionately to the poor? Near the close of the First World War, C. J. Kinne, a California layperson and publisher who eventually went to China himself to help build Bresee Memorial Hospital, wrote: "To love my neighbor is the test of whether or not I love God." Christians should seek to change social conditions not merely out of duty, Kinne believed, but out of love. "The church greatly needs this form of service in order to develop and increase the gift and graces which will make her Christ-like. If we are to be like our Lord, then we shall have to possess and exercise the same compassion and love which he had for all who were in distress." A religion, he said, "which does not flow out of the heart and life in streams of blessing unto needy souls is a poor thing in which to invest either time or money."[78] Accordingly, in the mid-1930s medical doctor Orpha Speicher built Reynolds Memorial Hospital in Washim, Maharashtra, India. Initially the hospital served women. Upon visiting the work in India some years later, General Superintendent Gideon B. Williamson agreed that training in cleanliness, hygiene, sanitation, literacy, and vocational arts validly accompanied the gospel. Unless basic needs were met, Williamson saw, converts were tempted to revert to old ways of life. "We must export not only the gospel of God's love and grace, but also Christian civilisation must be made to cover the earth as waters cover the sea."[79] The "primary purpose" of the church was "redemptive," but in carrying out this commission there was a large place for adequately preparing leaders, healing the sick, feeding the hungry, and giving water to the thirsty. "The points of ethics emphasized by the preachers of the social gospel have been included all along in the teaching of holiness," Williamson wrote in 1953.[80]

Likewise, David Hynd, born in Scotland and long-time missionary and medical doctor in Swaziland, believed that hospitals testified to the "regenerating power of the gospel with its spirit of divine compassion." Though Hynd could report many examples of conversions taking place at the church's hospital in Manzini, compassionate ministries, to him, were in themselves the "most effective interpretation of the Christ-like Spirit."[81] Hynd also spoke against the apartheid system in neighbouring South Africa.

The post-war church maintained hospitals in India and Swaziland, undertook responsibility for the International Holiness Mission's hospital in South Africa, and began a new hospital in Papua New Guinea. In India and Papua New Guinea, under the leadership of Carolyn Myatt, a nurse, community-based health care programs brought widespread change. In order to prevent disease, one had to deal with corporate, communal behaviour. Community-based health care and community-based holiness became integral as Nazarene hospitals and clinics were on the front lines of treating AIDS in these countries.[82]

In Bangladesh, the work of the church began in 1994 with compassionate ministries and schools integrated with other forms of evangelism in a country constantly wrecked by floods and famines. The Church of the Nazarene became the largest Protestant denomination in Bangladesh with 3,000 churches by 2016. One sees in compassion a wedding between the "cardinal" mission of the church, to preach the gospel, and the "distinguishing" mission of the church to proclaim (and embody) holiness.

Indigenous Leadership in Missions

While the church has been slow to do so in some places and at certain times in its history, it, nevertheless, developed strong local leaders. Global education played a key role in this, and missionaries saw their purpose, as William Esselstyn, missionary to South Africa said, "to help to build and train a corps of native workers who shall be able to carry on God's work in this land and to help prepare and publish holiness literature in the native languages."[83] Esselstyn's comment revealed the desire of the church not only to translate the holiness message in various cultures, but to make sure that it was understood.

Both Bresee and Reynolds favoured persons from their countries as key leaders. The People's Evangelical Church sent John Diaz back to his home country of Cape Verde in 1901. Diaz worked patiently in the town of Brava. In the early years he faced the active persecution not only of the Roman Catholic Church but of his own family. Once he was beaten nearly to death and converts were imprisoned. When Diaz established cordial relations with a priest, the situation improved. By 1921—after twenty years of work—Diaz had 100 converts, had opened a school, and had built a church seating 400. The Brava mayor and even a Roman Catholic priest occasionally attended the church.[84]

Other future leaders arrived on the doorstep of the Church of the Nazarene. In 1906, Bresee commissioned Sukhoda Banarjee and B. P. Biswas as missionaries to their home country of India. Banarjee's Hope School and Hallelujah Village in Calcutta, a mission for orphaned children, mostly girls, appealed strongly to Bresee. Three men who pioneered the Nazarene work in Japan, J. I. Nagamatsu, Hiroshi Kitagawa, and Nobumi Isayama, came into the church in California, and both Nagamatsu and Kitagawa graduated from the church's Pasadena College. Milhem Thahabeyah, a Syrian of Roman Catholic background, became the church's first missionary to his own country in 1920. Another early missionary, Samuel Krikorian, an Armenian, took the church to Palestine in 1921, where he worked among displaced Armenians. Soon after the Second World War, the church appointed Chung Nam Soo to lead the work in his home country of Korea. A. A. E. Berg became

District Superintendent in his home country of Australia in 1948, three years after the church opened work there. At about the same time, in Italy, Alfredo Del Rosso, a former Waldensian and Baptist, shepherded the congregations he had been leading into the Church of the Nazarene. Local leaders in Haiti and Samoa worked out less well in the long-term but provided the church its start in these countries.[85]

Meanwhile, the indigenisation of the work in such places as Mexico came about as much because of politics as strategy. The Holiness Church of Christ had established a mission in Chiapas, in southern Mexico in 1903. Missionary Carlos Miller opened the work in Mexico City a few years later. The government forced missionaries out in 1912, leaving the church in the hands of Vicente G. Santin. After hearing Miller preach, Santin, a Methodist local preacher as well as a medical doctor, sensed his need for a second work of grace. He testified to being sanctified and joined the Nazarene ministry. Santin became pastor of Mexico City First Church. Starting new churches was difficult. Law prohibited people from gathering in houses to worship. Nevertheless, during the year 1918, Santin preached 159 times, had 350 seekers, received 23 members, and, in his holistic ministry, treated 2,553 patients.[86]

In 1919, the General Superintendents appointed Santin District Superintendent. Aside from Scotsman George Sharpe, who had become district superintendent of the British Isles in 1915, Santin was the first national leader in such a position. Santin opened the Seminario Nazareno de Mexico. Out of the school came significant church leaders. H. T. Reza, Santin's son-in-law, said he was "a strict man, wise in counsel, fervent in payer, and above all, helpful to the end."[87]

Policies affirmed the goal of establishing strong local churches: "We must guard against the danger of keeping the native congregation in baby clothes too long. This will hinder the Holy Spirit in His freedom of operation among the people." Yet, the same 1923 Policy stated that it would be an error to release "our parental control over them before they are able to stand alone." Church leaders worried over "doctrinal confusion, and a low standard of experience."[88] If the church were to err, thought mission leaders, it would be better to err in keeping missionaries in control too long rather than in releasing national churches too quickly. Raising up converts not only saved and sanctified, but also prepared for leadership required Bible schools, and Nazarenes established these in nearly every country they entered.

To assure that converts would be worthy Nazarenes, for many years the practise in Swaziland was for the last day of a camp meeting to be set aside for the dedication of babies and the examination of candidates for membership. Those desiring membership first had to prove themselves faithful during two years of probation. Then a committee interrogated prospective members further for hours about their Christian walk. Could they testify to their conversion? Had they been tithing? Had they been a member of a missionary society? Had they fasted and prayed? Had they won other souls to Christ? Had they lived at peace with members of their family? If the committee was satisfied, these persons were joyously baptised and accepted as members.[89]

Study books written by Amy Hinshaw emphasised the roles of local "torch bearers." In Peru, and in other countries, the national workers faced far more likelihood of persecution and danger than might be found in eighteenth century Great Britain or nineteenth century North America. Nevertheless, leaders expected the same sort of loyalty to Christ's sacrifice that Wesley had expected of his local preachers and Asbury of his circuit riders. Victoriano Castaneda, for instance, itinerated and evangelised widely in the mountains of Peru. Once his home was burned to the ground and he barely escaped with his life. Another time, while holding a street meeting, a mob badly beat and nearly choked him to death.

Selling holiness books supported Nazarenes' itineration. People were more likely to read books that they had purchased than books that they had been given free. One early evangelist-colporteur in Peru was a woman, Natividad Herrara, who travelled by train and bus from town to town. She cooked with housewives while telling them about Christ. Even in places where they were settled, early pastors faced hostile crowds and persecution. The district of Llama, it seems, was especially hostile, as Amadeo Riguetti and Santiago Montoya both faced threats upon their lives while pastoring there.[90]

As in Mexico, political events in other countries necessitated drastic response. When the Japanese invaded Northern China in 1937, the Nazarene's most urgent priority was not evangelism but education. Ten years earlier the missionaries had fled during a wave of anti-foreignism; once again, it appeared they might have to flee again. Forty young men and women graduated from the Nazarene Bible College in 1940. After Pearl Harbor, the Japanese placed remaining missionaries in detention camps. Chinese pastors expanded the work inasmuch as they could under Japanese and then Communist governments. For the next fifty years, the Church of the Nazarene heard little about what was happening, but eventually realised that the Church had withstood turmoil and hardship, and had flourished, growing from 5,000 members in 1940 to more than 75,000 believers by 1989. When asked, in 1989, what the church might do to help, should it become possible, 69-year-old Shang Chih-rung, youngest of the 1940 class, said that the church was self-propagating, self-supporting, and self-governing. The missionaries had done their work well. They could be proud. He only wished for the same opportunities for education for his children and grandchildren as he himself had had.[91]

The Importance of Female Leadership

Around the world, women played significant roles in establishing and nurturing the Church; this included in China, where they itinerated as "Bible women." Women broke out of domestic spheres. With a band of women co-workers, Mary Lee Harris Cagle established churches in rural areas of the American southwest. The Holiness Church of Christ entered the union of 1908 with 31 ordained women. Later, with her second husband as District Superintendent, Cagle was the District Evangelist in New Mexico. On other districts as well, there was a similar arrangement, with the husband as District Superintendent and the wife as district evangelist.[92]

Beginning in Bresee's time, in 1904, Mae McReynolds initiated missions to Hispanics in Los Angeles. Ordained in 1906, she expanded her ministry from Southern California to Texas. She was seated as a superintendent in general assemblies. One of the fruits of her ministry, Santos Elizondo planted churches in the vicinity of El Paso, Texas, and Juarez, Mexico, where she also maintained an orphanage. In Argentina, an outstanding leader was Lucia Carmen Garcia de Costa, the church's first convert in the country, and in 1931 among the first Nazarenes to be ordained. She evangelised, planted, and pastored churches. Garcia received a PhD in linguistics and taught in the Nazarene Bible Institute while translating holiness books from English to Spanish.[93]

Women missionaries often outnumbered men two-to-one. The church sent out a single woman or two alongside a husband and wife. Women served in traditional roles of teachers and nurses, but also in non-traditional roles as doctors and evangelists. Mary Cooper, in her 42-year career in Mozambique, evangelised over thousands of miles and at one time superintended 90 churches. Lorraine Schultz taught in the Bible school at Tavane and educated a generation of Mozambique ministers. Cooper and Schultz were examples to Mozambique women such as Bessie Tshambe, whose Central Church in Maputo, Mozambique numbered over 1,500 in the 1990s.[94] Similarly, in Japan, missionaries such as Minnie Staples and Mildred Bangs Wynkoop stood in the historical background of the election of Motoko Matsuda, a woman, as district superintendent in 2007. She pastored the Kura Church of the Nazarene near Hiroshima. General Superintendent Nina Gunter was presiding when the Japan district assembly elected Matsuda as District Superintendent.[95]

The first women to lead Nazarene colleges were on mission fields. These included Jeanine van Beek, a Dutch woman who had immigrated to Australia, where she graduated from the Nazarene Bible College in Sydney. After pastoring a church in Germany, van Beek taught at European Nazarene Bible College in Büsingen, Germany. In 1975, she went to Haiti, where she served as rector of the Nazarene theological college. In 1990 she returned to European Nazarene Bible College as rector and served till 1998.[96] In 2005, another female rector of European Nazarene Bible College, Corlis McGee, became the first female president of Eastern Nazarene College in the USA. We have also had female college leaders in many other countries: Leah Marangu was appointed vice chancellor of African Nazarene University in Kenya in 1996; Winnie Nhlengethwa was installed as the first Vice Chancellor of Southern Africa Nazarene University 2010; and in 2012, Deirdre Brower Latz became principal of Nazarene Theological College in Manchester, England.

In the Church of the Nazarene, men view women as co-workers of equal dignity and respect. Section 501 of the 2017-2021 *Manual* of the Church of the Nazarene expresses a "Theology of Women in Ministry." "The Church of the Nazarene supports the right of women to use their God-given spiritual gifts within the church and affirms the historic right of women to be elected and appointed to places of leadership within the Church of the Nazarene, including the offices of both elder and deacon." Biblical foundations as well as theological premises rest behind this statement. There are many examples in both the Old and New Testaments of the leadership of women. Christ came to reverse the social inequalities between men and woman created by the Fall. Paul affirms that in Christ there is "neither male nor female" (Galatians 3:28). All stand on equal footing before the cross of Christ. All are one "in Christ." Concerning other statements by Paul that seem to limit women's role in the church, the Church of the Nazarene understands that these are related to specific situations in specific places at specific times and that they do not relate to the Church in all places at all times.[97]

DISCUSSION QUESTIONS

1. What do you see as the pluses and minuses of both Reynolds's and Bresee's understanding of missions and the organisational models they produced?

2. Does holiness manifest itself in the same ways across cultures? How is it manifested in your cultural setting? Can holiness be organisationally "structured"?

3. How has Nazarene Global Missions impacted your country, your district, your local church, your personal life? What has been the influence of indigenous leaders?

4. Is compassion an end in itself or a means of evangelism? How has your local church viewed Compassionate Ministries and Missions/evangelism? As united or separate?

5. Did anything surprise you about the role of women in the Church of the Nazarene?

6. How does our position on women in leadership distinguish us from some other denominations? Why is it such an important part of our identity and theological identity?

CHAPTER 5

EDUCATION IN THE CHURCH OF THE NAZARENE

In going to a lost world, the primary objective of our Nazarene schools was spiritual: the salvation of sinners, the sanctification of believers. The means of accomplishing this goal was by organising "Christians into churches and training them to the point of establishing an indigenous church,"[98] and the schools were the primary means of training pastors so as to enable truly indigenous, self-propagating churches. To bear such fruit, the church's roots needed to be deep. The Church of the Nazarene built its ministerial education program upon the assumption that pastors must possess a wide spectrum of knowledge in order to understand and to communicate to their context and to the current generation. Almost as soon as Nazarenes entered a new country, they established schools for educating pastors and Christian workers.

Twenty years ago, the General Superintendents issued a defining document that indicated the church's "core values" as Christian, holiness, and missional. Therein, they stated that: "We are committed to Christian education. ... We are committed to the pursuit of knowledge, the development of Christian character, and the equipping of leaders to accomplish our God-given calling of serving in the church and in the world."[99]

Education for the World

Started in 1899 with A. M. Hills as its first president, Texas Holiness University, forerunner of Southern Nazarene University in Bethany, Oklahoma, typified early Nazarene education. School leaders typically have been, like Hills, well-educated, yet, at the same time, preachers of holiness. While raising money for the schools, they have served with pastoral hearts. Teachers, sensing their own calling, have been so loyal to the church that they have accepted low salaries, heavy teaching loads, and *pro bono* administrative responsibilities. When faculty members published, it has often been for the church, not for the scholarly guild. Furthermore, Texas Holiness University, Pacific Bible College under Phineas Bresee, and other early Nazarene schools, welcomed those of any denomination.

Bresee hoped in establishing Pacific Bible College, which became Pasadena College and, later, Point Loma Nazarene University, that it would attract students from many denominations. The school announced in 1902 that it was "not sectarian, but is in the broad sense Christian," and "seeks not sectarianism but Bible culture for all men and women who may desire to avail themselves of its advantages."[100] Nazarenes wanted their education to be so appealing, and affordable, that young people from other traditions and from all economic strata would come. Nazarenes did not demand conformity to their Articles of Faith either for entry into their schools or for graduation but expected that young people would walk out of their doors not only with diplomas but with deeply consecrated hearts.[101]

Students heard the message of holiness in chapels and classrooms. Hills, for instance, fully described the Calvinist position on issues, but every student knew where their professor stood. Among Texas Holiness University graduates were Roy T. Williams and J. B. Chapman, both taught by Hills, both his successors as head of the school, and both eventually General Superintendents. Like all Nazarene schools, the curriculum of Texas Holiness University was broad. There was no fear of philosophy or science, the school taught classical music and literature, and required its graduates to learn Latin, Greek, modern languages, and mathematics alongside the Bible.

Like many of the other schools in the USA, Eastern Nazarene College (ENC), in Quincy, Massachusetts, the church's second oldest college, offered various majors, mathematics to music, physics to philosophy. All students took core subjects in religion, humanities, social sciences, and natural sciences. Through a committee that formulated a "Philosophy of Education," adopted by the 1952 General Assembly, long-term ENC Academic Dean Bertha Munro embedded a philosophy of liberal arts in the Church of the Nazarene. The church expected schools to provide the denomination with "a ministry which shall be orthodox in belief, sound in Christian experience, trustworthy in example, wise in counsel, and efficient in practice; and with a laity who shall be intelligent and clear-thinking, loyal to the sacred mission of a holiness church, devoted and earnest—ministry and laity adjusted in a working unit, with a vision of world needs and a warmth of love for Christ and His kingdom." The objective was "a fusion of holy character and sound education."[102]

The Spirit at work in the mind and heart of theologians, enabling theologians to pursue and to understand truth by means of revelation, enabled scientists to pursue and to understand truth by means of reason. Should knowledge appear in conflict with faith, Nazarenes could rest assured that there was one truth. If, at the end of any class period, whether the subject was Bible, Sociology, or Biology, students had doubts, they had the right to ask their lecturer how they integrated what they had just taught with their own personal faith. The same lecturers gathered around students at kneeling rails during revival meetings or following chapel messages.[103]

Nearly all of the church's early leaders and missionaries attended schools with this sort of character and took with them the importance of a broad curriculum in the education of leaders. Such missionaries included Harmon Schmelzenbach, the pioneer missionary to Swaziland, who was studying at Texas Holiness University and reading about the missionary to Africa, David Livingstone, when the story stopped him. He kneeled, praying, "Lord, here am I: send me to tell them. ... The burden for Africa rolled upon his heart, filled his eyes with tears of compassion, and started his mind thinking in terms of getting to the field of service as soon as possible."[104] Before graduating, in the Spring of 1907 Schmelzenbach left for Africa. Leighton S. Tracy and Gertrude Tracy had just graduated from Pentecostal Collegiate Institute when they sailed for India in 1904. Both Kagawa in Japan and Krikorian in Palestine were graduates of Pasadena. Thahabiyah in Syria, William Eckel in Japan, Evelyn Witthoff in India, and Mary Scott in China were graduates of Olivet. Louise Robinson Chapman studied at Northwest Nazarene College, as did John Pattee, who served in China and the Philippines. While furloughed during the Second World War, Pattee, known as an evangelist, earned an MA at Pasadena College. The list goes on. The church around the world, as a result, did not fear education or sense that education threatened faith.

Nazarenes did not erect liberal arts colleges abroad, as they had in the USA. Likewise, they did not establish short-term, fast-track training schools. Rather, the model was rigorous three-year and four-year programs, often at the university level. While Nazarenes craved Spirit-filled ministers, they expected that they had studied God's Word. The curricula of the Bible colleges included literature, philosophy, sociology, psychology, and science as well as Bible, church history, theology, and pastoral ministry, all requisite for ordination in the Church of the Nazarene.[105]

With Matthew 28:18-20 as the church's "Great Commission," Nazarenes eagerly went to evangelise the world as quickly as possible. The harvest was ripe, and there was little time. After the Second World War, Cold War tensions contributed to expectations about Christ's soon return. Yet the Communist take-over of China, Cuba, and Mozambique also demonstrated the importance of preparing local leaders. Esselstyn emphasised, in Africa, that if all the church's money and effort were in evangelism, there would be shallow faith and commitment.[106] Similarly, Williamson admonished, "Those who have engaged in evangelism and have neglected to conduct a program of education have discovered that it was all but impossible to accomplish abiding results."[107] In Japan, Wynkoop believed that only through education could the Japanese address the complex issues of their culture. To break through Shintoism, she observed in 1963, "educational muscles and bones" must support the "evangelistic arm" of the church.[108]

Nazarene schools prepared both pastors and laypersons to reach the highest levels of society with confidence. A few of our theological colleges endeavoured to provide PhDs in various theological disciplines as a way of training up the next generation of theological educators. Nazarene Theological College in Manchester, England succeeded in this by linking itself to University of Manchester and Nazarene Theological College in Brisbane, Australia, through its connection with the ecumenical consortium of Sydney College of Divinity.

Still, the real mission of the church was not to the highest but to the lowest segments of society. No matter the competency of its scholars, the holiness message compelled Nazarenes to go to the neglected quarters of the world, to the poorest of the poor of whom Jesus spoke, the seemingly insignificant ones: "See that you do not look down on one of these little ones" (Matthew 18). The Wesleyan heritage gave Nazarenes a kind of homing instinct toward those without advantages in society; it communicated an ethos of Christ-like service and perfect love. Knowledge of Christian beliefs and doctrines, combined with a sanctified heart produced a purity of love that incited toward action among the poorest of the poor.

How did education fit within the broader mission of preaching holiness to the poor? In Kenya, Africa Nazarene University prepares undergraduates in computer science as well as master's students in the contextualisation of holiness for Africa. Southern Africa Nazarene University in Swaziland resulted from the merger of the School of Nursing with the Teachers' College and the theological college. Over 100 years, Nazarenes made a great impact upon the educational and medical systems of Swaziland. The church has had a comparable impact on the highlands of Papua New Guinea through its Nursing College and health care program. In Korea, the Nazarene University grew out of the theological college and under Presidents William Patch and Seung-an Im emphasised rehabilitation studies for those with disabilities, an area that fit the Nazarene concern for those neglected and shunned in society. The theological college in Trinidad offered master's degrees in social work and counselling as well as theology. The two Nazarene colleges in the Philippines offered degrees in education that allowed graduates to teach in public schools. In the same country, Asia-Pacific Nazarene Theological Seminary became well known for its programs in holistic child development. Trevecca Nazarene University in Nashville, Tennessee, once a segregated school, now has a Centre for Social Justice. Often those outside of the Church of the Nazarene know the denomination only by its schools and their programs, not by its teachings or doctrines.

Conclusion

In Romans 10:2, the Apostle Paul criticised Jews for having zeal without knowledge. Once Paul himself was such a Jew. Paul was remembering Proverb 19:2, "It is not good to have zeal without knowledge, nor be hasty and miss the way." Nazarenes embraced these sentiments and have been deliberate rather than hasty in the education of ministers. While Nazarenes craved Spirit-filled ministers, they expected that ministers had studied God's Word, and that they understood theology, church history, Christian education, and the practical arts of ministry.

That there was no conflict between the deepest Christian piety and the highest academic attainment went back to Wesley. Himself an Oxford graduate, he did not demand college degrees of his preachers, but did require that they read deeply in Christian faith and learn Hebrew and Greek as well as proper English. When, in 1748, John Wesley started Kingswood School for the children of his traveling preachers, Charles Wesley, his brother, wrote this verse:

Error and ignorance remove, their blindness both of heart and mind;
Give them the wisdom from above, spotless, and peaceable, and kind;
In knowledge pure their minds renew, and store with thoughts divinely true . . .
Unite the pair so oft disjoined, knowledge and vital piety;
Learning and holiness combined, and truth and love, let all men see
In those, whom up to Thee we give, Thine, wholly Thine, to die and live.

Uniting "the pair so oft disjoined, knowledge and vital piety" has been the on-going goal of education in the Nazarene tradition.

DISCUSSION QUESTIONS

1. How does education play into our core values of being Christian, Holiness, and Missional?

2. What has been the purpose of Nazarene schools? How have Nazarene schools shaped you and/or your local church?

3. Why is it important to have well-educated ministers who are committed to being life-long learners?

4. Why is it important to have a well-educated laity who have a Christian worldview and a Nazarene DNA?

CHAPTER 6

COMMUNION WITH CHRIST

At the 1960 General Assembly, General Superintendent Hugh C. Benner preached a sermon entitled "Pattern for Survival"; the text was Revelation 3:14-22. Benner warned Nazarenes gathered that warm June night that they must not become like the Laodicean church. The Church of the Nazarene had celebrated its fiftieth anniversary two years earlier. The world was in the midst of a cold war between the Soviet Union and the USA. Benner asked the Church of the Nazarene to consider what it would take to survive as the peculiar church that God had called it to be. It was not just John's controversy with the Laodicea church, it was God's controversy with the Church of the Nazarene that prompted Benner's sermon.[109]

The Divine Controversy

Benner described the divine controversy—the controversy between God and his Church. Laodicea was the richest of the seven cities to which John spoke; it was a trading and banking centre and was made up of many Jewish Christians. Yet the church in Laodicea lacked full devotion to God and his work. Instead, formalism had entered into the church (not unlike the formalism that had entered into the Church of England during Wesley's time, and into the Methodist Church in America during Bresee's). The church possessed routines without life. The church was neither hot nor cold. It was indifferent, possessed by an emotionless religion with no heart and no feeling. Once its members had been filled with zeal. Once there had been vitality in their Christian witness and testimony. Once there had been passion. Now it was gone.

But why did Benner preach this sermon to the faithful Nazarene crowd gathered in 1960? The founders of the church had passed away. Had their zeal also passed away? Had the Church of the Nazarene become lukewarm? Did it possess only lifeless routines? Was it losing its passion? Those who attended—pastors of large and small churches, district superintendents, Sunday school superintendents and teachers, young people's society leaders, missionary society presidents, local church board members—could remember the church's poverty during the 1930s and the darkness of the early 1940s. During those days Nazarenes had lived meagrely. They had sacrificed much, praying and fasting and giving beyond their means to keep the colleges open. Women had placed their jewellery on kneeling rails, to be sold in order to keep missionaries on the field. Then, from the late 1940s, prosperity had come. The colleges they had struggled to keep open had produced graduates who were good tithing laypersons. They did not need to sacrifice as much to keep the schools open and to expand missions. At the same time, Nazarenes had joined the mainstream of culture. They were not so peculiar as before. They had become respectable. But, spiritually speaking, Benner asked, was the church not still "blind, poor, and naked"?

The church in Laodicea had lost its spiritual reality and had become a religion without the touch of God, a going through the motions. The church had lost communion with God. Yes, they were doctrinally orthodox and well organized. Yes, the church machinery cranked on. But was there love? Spiritual joy? Radiance? They hold church, they have their Sunday schools, they have their young people's society meetings, they have their missionary meetings, and they have their church board meetings. They have their fellowships, they pray, they sing, they praise, and they worship. The church goes on—with or without the Spirit of God. Benner worried as to the state of the Church of the Nazarene in 1960. Was Christ in the midst? If not, did anyone notice? What was the answer to this lukewarm-ness? The only hope was to commit anew to Jesus Christ and be, as John said, "gold tried in the fire." Would the church be willing to go through fire in order to be pure?

The Divine Communion

Benner desired divine communion for the church. Christ was knocking at the door of the church, he said. Nazarenes thought of this verse and this image as one of Christ knocking on the heart-door of unbelievers. But, really, said Benner, the text was written to the church! Christ will not force himself in. The latch is on the inside. He would come in if invited. Was Christ knocking on the door of the Church of the Nazarene? Would anyone hear his knock? If Jesus comes into his church, Benner said, he will clear out the barriers just as he cleared away the money-changers at the temple, those who made church into a business. Jesus was able to clear any of the barriers limiting or shutting God out. These are the barriers of "carnal indifference" and "carnal disobedience," which are quenching the Spirit.

The application of the word "carnal" to those good church leaders gathered at the 1960 General Assembly must have been quite a shock to them. These were devoted people, many of them privileged to have been elected to the General Assembly. They had taken the time and effort to attend. The best of the best Nazarenes; they were not "sinners." In fact, they could stand and testify to the time and place where Christ had sanctified them. Yet, Benner called the church he was addressing "carnal." Of the flesh? Unsanctified? Could they not count on their having had a spiritual experience at some time and place that cleansed their carnality? The real question was whether they were there and then living in obedience to and fellowship with the Spirit. Once they were tender to Christ's leading. Once they were sensitive to his convicting Spirit. Once they were zealous. Had they grown apart from Christ? Only if they were humble enough to recognise their carnality would they be moved toward repentance. If they kept thinking that they were holy or felt as if they needed to keep up the impression that they were, they would never come to repentance.

Benner's sermon conveyed concern that in the transition from being a movement to a well-organized church, something might have been lost. Still, Christ was knocking at the door of his Church. He desired to share his divine communion. He invited his friends to share with him his divine presence. When Jesus came in, he melted the barriers between ourselves and God. He healed. He sanctified. When Jesus came in he changed carnal indifference into a passionate desire to serve him. When Jesus came in he brought the promise of overcoming the world; he brought the promise of overcoming ourselves. When Jesus came in he brought divine resources. He brought his power into his people. He brought evangelistic effectiveness. He brought creativity. He brought compassion. He brought his Spirit.

Conclusion

That same Christ who walked alongside Cleopas and his friend on the road to Emmaus, has been walking and talking alongside the Church of the Nazarene. He has shown us about ourselves as well as himself. During the post-resurrection appearances of Jesus, the Scriptures record several times that he ate with his disciples. He was eating with them when he told them to wait in Jerusalem for the promised Holy Spirit. More than that, across the three years since he had called his disciples, he had broken bread with them nearly every day. So it happened that when he broke bread with Cleopas and his friend on the road to Emmaus they realised it was him. They saw the marks of the nails on his hands when he broke the bread.

Likewise, he is here; not only to walk and talk alongside us, and to reveal his very presence, but also, as he did with those two friends, to break bread. We ask, how has Christ been talking to us? How is he talking to us just now? The Church of the Nazarene is growing in maturity. In a global web of ever-changing social, political, and economic forces, we are still in the process of becoming what we are intended to be. We have not arrived. We are a people still on a walk with Christ. As he did when he talked with the two disciples on the road to Emmaus, Jesus is walking alongside and talking to the Church of the Nazarene. He is opening us to Scriptures, talking about his Kingdom, and pointing us to himself. May we be ever willing to hear his voice, to open the door and invite him in, and to enter into divine communion with him daily together as his Church.

DISCUSSION QUESTIONS

1. In what ways are you still in a process of discovery? In what ways is your local church still in a process of discovery?

2. How does knowing the larger history of the Church of the Nazarene help you move into a closer future with God? What do you know of your own local church's history and what practical things can this teach you?

SUGGESTION FOR FURTHER READING

Beginner

Bangs, Carl. *Phineas F. Bresee: His Life in Methodism, the Holiness Movement, and the Church of the Nazarene.* Kansas City: Beacon Hill, 1995.

Cunningham, Floyd T. *Holiness Abroad: Nazarene Missions in Asia.* Lanham, MD: Scarecrow, 2003.

Ingersol, Stan. *Nazarene Roots: Pastors, Prophets, Revivalists & Reformers.* Kansas City: Beacon Hill, 2009.

Laird, Rebecca. *Ordained Women in the Church of the Nazarene: The First Generation.* Kansas City: Nazarene Publishing House, 1993.

Tracy, Wesley and Stan Ingersol. *What is a Nazarene? Understanding Our Place in the Religious Community.* Kansas City: Beacon Hill, 1998.

Intermediate to Advanced

Branstetter, C. J. *Purity, Power, and Pentecostal Light: The Revivalist Doctrine and Means of Aaron Merritt Hills.* Eugene, OR: Pickwick, 2012.

Cunningham, Floyd T., et al. *Our Watchword and Song: The Centennial History of the Church of the Nazarene.* Kansas City: Beacon Hill, 2009.

Dieter, Melvin. *The Holiness Revival of the Nineteenth Century.* Second ed. Lanham, MD: Scarecrow, 1996.

Ellis, Dirk R. *Holy Fire Fell: A History of Worship, Revivals, and Feasts in the Church of the Nazarene.* Eugene, OR: Wipf & Stock, 2016.

Reed, Rodney. *Holy with Integrity: The Unity of Personal and Social Ethics in the Holiness Movement, 1880-1910.* Salem, OH: Schmul, 2003.

Shea, Mary Lou. *In Need of Your Prayers and Patience: The Life and Ministry of Hiram F. Reynolds and the Founding of the Church of the Nazarene*. Eugene, OR: Resource, 2015.

Smith, Timothy L. *Called Unto Holiness: The Story of the Nazarenes: The Formative Years*. Kansas City: Nazarene, 1962.

NOTES

1 H. Orton Wiley, *Christian Theology*, vol. 1 (Kansas City: Nazarene, 1940), 3.
2 William Greathouse, "Foreword," to *Holiness Teaching – New Testament Times to Wesley*, edited by Paul M. Bassett (Kansas City: Beacon Hill, 1997), 11.
3 See Wade Clark Roof, *Spiritual Marketplace: Baby Boomers and the Remaking of American Religion* (Princeton: Princeton U. Press, 1999).
4 *Association of Pentecostal Churches of America: Minutes of the Twelfth Annual Meeting* (Providence, RI: Pentecostal Printing, 1907), 3-4, 5, 12, 15, 17.
5 Jack Ford, *In the Steps of John Wesley: The Church of the Nazarene in Britain* (Kansas City: Nazarene, 1968), 155; Floyd T. Cunningham, Holiness Abroad: Nazarene Missions in Asia (Lanham, MD: Scarecrow, 2003), 72-74.
6 For the Free Methodist Church in Texas see C. B. Jernigan, *Pioneer Days*, 86-90. See also Howard Snyder, *Populist Saints*: B. T. and Ellen Roberts and the First Free Methodists (Grand Rapids: Eerdmans, 2006), 520-523, and throughout.
7 D. S. Warner and H. M. Riggle, *The Cleansing of the Sanctuary or, The Church of God in Type and Antitype, and in Prophecy and Revelation* (1903; reprint, Guthrie, OK: Faith Publishing House, 1967), 262, 268. See John W. V. Smith, *The Quest for Holiness and Unity: A Centennial History of the Church of God* (Anderson, Indiana) (Anderson, IN: Warner Press, 1980), xiii-xiv, 54-57, 75-76.
8 A. B. Simpson, *The Four-Fold Gospel* (Harrisburg, PA: Christian Publications, 1925); Lettie B. Cowman, Charles E. Cowman, Missionary: Warrior (Los Angeles: Oriental Missionary Society, [1928]), 231-247; Dieter, *The Holiness Revival*, 207-230; Donald Dayton, *Theological Roots of Pentecostalism* (Grand Rapids: Zondervan, 1987), 106-108, 175-176; Meesaeng Lee Choi, *The Rise of the Korean Holiness Church in Relation to the American Holiness Movement: Wesley's "Scriptural Holiness" and the "Fourfold Gospel"* (Lanham, MD: Scarecrow, 2008).
9 *Echoes of the General Holiness Assembly, Held in Chicago, May 3-13, 1901*, ed. S. B. Shaw (Chicago: S. B. Shaw, [1901]), 274-275.
10 John Wesley, "Minutes of Several Conversations between the Rev. Mr. *Wesley and Others*," *The Works of John Wesley*, Jackson edition (Reprint, Kansas City: Beacon Hill, 1979), 8: 299.
11 Robert Lee Harris, *Why We Left the M.E. Church, South* (N.p., [1894]), 15.
12 Phineas Bresee, *Sermons from Matthew's Gospel* (Kansas City: Nazarene, n.d.), 96.
13 *The Certainties of Faith: Ten Sermons by the Founder of the Church of the Nazarene*, ed. Timothy L. Smith (Kansas City: Nazarene, 1958), 27. See Dirk R. Ellis, *Holy Fire Fall: A History of Worship, Revivals, and Feasts in the Church of the Nazarene* (Eugene: Wipf & Stock, 2016).

14 John N. Short, sermon to the 1906 Assembly of the Church of the Nazarene in Los Angeles, as recorded by Hulda Grebe, "Minutes of the Assembly, October 3, 1906," *Merging Religious Bodies* microfilm Reel 2.

15 Phineas Bresee, "The Gift of Tongues," *Nazarene Messenger*, December 13, 1906, 6.

16 Smith, "Introduction," to *The Certainties of Faith*, 11.

17 Bresee, *Sermons from Matthew's Gospel*, 131. See E. A. Girvin, *Phineas Bresee: A Prince in Israel: A Biography* (Kansas City: Nazarene, 1916), 108, 133-142.

18 Phineas Bresee, "History of the Church of the Nazarene," *Nazarene Messenger* (July 4, 1907).

19 Bresee, *Sermons from Matthew*, 60.

20 Bresee, *Sermons on Isaiah*, 118. See Donald P. Brickley, *Man of the Morning: The Life and Work of Phineas F. Bresee* (Kansas City: Nazarene, 1960), 153-161.

21 *Association of Pentecostal Churches of America Minutes of the Tenth Annual Meeting* (Providence, RI: Pentecostal Printing Company, 1905), 49. See *Proceedings of the First General Assembly of the Pentecostal Church of the Nazarene* (Los Angeles: [Pentecostal Church of the Nazarene], 1907), 23-24, 47. See also Cunningham, *Holiness Abroad*, 11-14, 57-63.

22 *Minutes of the Missionary Committee of the Association of Pentecostal Churches of America*, June 27, 1906. See Hiram F. Reynolds, *"The Missionary Work,"* May 23, 1907. See Carl Bangs, *Phineas F. Bresee: His Life in Methodism, the Holiness Movement, and the Church of the Nazarene* (Kansas City: Beacon Hill, 1995), 187-188, 200, 218, 227.

23 *Association of Pentecostal Churches of America Minutes of the Tenth Annual Meeting*, 14.

24 Phineas Bresee, "Our Church Polity," *Herald of Holiness*, June 5, 1912.

25 In 1989, the church constituted the order of "deacon" – open to women and now, also, to men. Deacons were full-time ordained ministers who also had completed a pre-determined Course of Study.

26 Smith, *Called Unto Holiness*, 216, 220. See Bangs, *Bresee*, 187, 188, and 200, for the middle-class orientation of Bresee's congregation in Los Angeles.

27 C. B. Jernigan, *Pioneer Days of the Holiness Movement in the Southwest* (Kansas City: Nazarene, 1919), 150-157; Melvin E. Dieter, *The Holiness Revival of the Nineteenth Century*, second edition (Lanham, MD: Scarecrow, 1996), 199-246.

28 Phineas Bresee, "History of the Church of the Nazarene," *Nazarene Messenger* (July 4, 1907). See Stan Ingersol, "Christian Baptism and the Early Nazarenes: The Sources that Shaped a Pluralistic Baptismal Tradition," *Wesleyan Theological Journal* 27 (Spring-Fall 1992), 161-180.

29 See various articles in the April 17, 1912, April 24, 1912, and May 1, 1912 issues of the *Herald of Holiness*. See Randall J. Stephens, *The Fire Spreads: holiness and Pentecostalism in the American South* (Cambridge, MA: Harvard U. Press, 2008), 173-185. On the organisation of holiness denominations as part of the search for order see Dieter, *The Holiness Revival*, 255-265.

30 E.g., *Proceedings of the First General Assembly*, 57-58; *Proceedings of the Second General Assembly of the Pentecostal Church of the Nazarene* (Los Angeles: Nazarene, 1908), 46-47. See Bresee's sermons "Righteousness in Politics,"

and "Holiness and Civic Righteousness," in *Sermons on Isaiah* (Kansas City: Nazarene, 1926), 61-69, 79-87. Smith, *Called unto Holiness*, 36-37, 161-162, 203-204, and 266-271, emphasises the churchly character. On the Church of the Nazarene as a "believer's church" see Stan Ingersol, *Past and Prospect: The Promise of Nazarene History* (San Diego: Point Loma Press, 2014), 19-20.

31 *Manual of the Pentecostal Church of the Nazarene Published by Authority of the General Assembly Held at Pilot Point, Texas 1908* (Los Angeles: Nazarene, 1908), 26, 32, 35-38, 70-74; Smith, *Called unto Holiness*, 115, 216, 220. For tobacco use among Methodists in the late nineteenth century in the South see Ted Ownby, *Subduing Satan: Religion, Recreation, and Manhood in the Rural South, 1865-1920* (Chapel Hill: U. of North Carolina Press, 1990), 132-134, and Briane K. Turley, *A Wheel within a Wheel: Southern Methodism and the Georgia Holiness Association* (Macon, GA: Mercer U. Press, 1999), 164-165.

32 *Holiness Association Year Book 1906-1907* (N.p., [1907]), 67-69. Also see M. Brandon Winstead, *There All Along: Black Participation in the Church of the Nazarene 1914-1969* (Lexington, KY: Emeth, 2012).

33 *Manual of the People's Evangelical Church of Providence, R.I.* (Providence: Beulah Christian, 1895), 6; *Constitution of the Association of Pentecostal Churches of America* (Providence: Beulah Christian, 1897), 10.

34 Cunningham et al, *Our Watchword and Song: The Centennial History of the Church of the Nazarene* (Kansas City: Beacon Hill, 2009), 234-41.

35 Smith, *Called Unto Holiness*, 296.

36 "Quadrennial Address," *Journal of the Tenth General Assembly of the Church of the Nazarene*, eds. C. Warren Jones and Mendall Taylor (N.p., [1940]), 205, 207, 216-217, 220.

37 *Quadrennial Reports to the Eleventh General Assembly of the Church of the Nazarene* (N. p., [1944]), 75, 102; Jones, "A Plain Statement of Facts," *Other Sheep* (March 1947), 1. See "The Woman's Foreign Missionary Society of the Church of the Nazarene," 12 [1948] (Nazarene Archives, file 423-7); *Herald of Holiness* (February 11, 1959), 3-4.

38 Mendell Taylor, *Exploring Evangelism* (Kansas City: Beacon Hill, 1964), 7. See also Howard A. Snyder, *The Problem of Wineskins: Church Structure in a Technological Age* (Downer's Grove, IL: Inter-Varsity Press, 1975).

39 Bresee, *Sermons on Isaiah*, 46.

40 See, for instance, Wynkoop, *John Wesley: Christian Revolutionary* (Kansas City: Beacon Hill, 1970); Raymond Hurn, *Mission Possible: A Study of the Mission of the Church of the Nazarene* (Kansas City: Nazarene, 1973); R. Franklin Cook and Stephen Weber, *The Greening: The Story of Nazarene Compassionate Ministries* (Kansas City: Nazarene, 1986); Howard Culbertson, *The Kingdom Strikes Back: Signs of the Messiah at Work in Haiti* (Kansas City: Nazarene, 1990).

41 Quoted in W. E. Sangster, *The Path to Perfection: An Examination and Restatement of John Wesley's Doctrine of Christian Perfection* (New York: Abingdon-Cokesbury, 1943), 59. See Franz Hildebrandt and Oliver A. Beckerlegge, eds., *The Works of John Wesley, vol. 7: A Collection of Hymns for the Use of the People Called Methodists* (Nashville: Abingdon, 1983), 322-333.

42 Editorial, *Herald of Holiness* (December 18, 1912), 3.

43 Bresee, "History of the Church of the Nazarene," *Nazarene Messenger* (July 4, 1907).

44 The Church of the Nazarene reprinted Palmer's *The Way of Holiness and other writings*.

45 Charles G. Finney, *The Promise of the Spirit*, compiled and edited by Timothy L. Smith (Minneapolis: Bethany, 1980).

46 See Warren, *O for a Thousand Tongues*, 98-113.

47 Basil Miller, *Bud Robinson: Miracle of Grace* (Kansas City: Beacon Hill, 1947), 76. See Robinson, *Sunshine and Smiles: Life Story, Flash Lights, Sayings and Sermons* (Chicago: Christian Witness, 1903), 38-70.

48 D. Shelby Corlett, *Spirit-Filled: The Life of the Rev. James Blaine Chapman* (Kansas City: Beacon Hill, n.d.), 34.

49 Hills, "Foreword" to *Fundamental Christian Theology: A Systematic Theology*, vol. 1 (Pasadena: C. J. Kinne, 1931), 5.

50 *Manual of the Pentecostal Church of the Nazarene* (Los Angeles: Nazarene, [1908]), 27.

51 Hills, *Fundamental Christian Theology*, vol. 1: 370; vol. 2: 325-330, 339-360.

52 Article IV, *Nazarene Manual*; Wiley, *Christian Theology*, vol. 1 (Kansas City: Beacon Hill, 1943), 454-456.

53 Louis A. Reed, "The Counselor's Corner," *Preacher's Magazine*, May-June 1950, 5-6.

54 Lewis T. Corlett, *Holiness, the Harmonizing Experience* (Kansas City: Beacon Hill, 1952), 68. See Corlett, "Holiness and Nervous Reactions," in *Further Insights into Holiness: Nineteen Leading Wesleyan Scholars Present Various Phases of Holiness Thinking*, comp. Kenneth Geiger (Kansas City: Beacon Hill, 1963), 333-349, and Corlett, *Thank God and Take Courage: How the Holy Spirit Worked in My Life*, ed. Frank Carver (San Diego: Point Loma Press, 1992), 34-37.

55 Grider, *Entire Sanctification: The Distinctive Doctrine of Wesleyanism* (Kansas City: Beacon Hill, 1980), 105-113, 125-130.

56 See William Greathouse, *From the Apostles to Wesley* (Kansas City: Nazarene, 1979); Paul Bassett and William Greathouse, *Exploring Christian Holiness*, volume two, *The Historical Development* (Kansas City: Nazarene, 1985); and *Great Holiness Classics*, vol. 1: *Holiness Teaching: New Testament Times to Wesley* (Kansas City: Nazarene, 1997), edited (and for the most part translated from original texts) by Paul Bassett.

57 Mildred Bangs Wynkoop, *A Theology of Love: The Dynamic of Wesleyanism* (Kansas City: Beacon Hill, 1972), 47-52.

58 "Upon Our Lord's Sermon on the Mount: Tenth Discourse," *The Works of John Wesley*, vol. 1: Sermons, 662; "A Plain Account of Christian Perfection," Works, 3rd ed., 11: 367-368, 441.

59 "Salvation by Faith," *The Works of John Wesley*, vol. 1: Sermons, ed. Outler, 125.

60 Smith, *Revivalism and Social Reform: American Protestantism on the Eve of the Civil War* (Reprint, New York: Harper and Row, 1965), 175-176.

61 Smith, "Introduction," to Finney, *The Promise of the Spirit*, 13.

62 David O. Moberg, *The Great Reversal: Evangelism and Social Concern* (Philadelphia: J. B. Lippincott, 1972); Jean Miller Schmidt, "Reexamining

the Public/Private Split: Reforming the Continent and Spreading Scriptural Holiness," in *Rethinking Methodist History: A Bicentennial Historical Consultation*, eds. Russell E. Richey and Kenneth Rowe (Nashville: Kingswood, 1985), 75-80.

63   Hurn, *Mission Possible: A Study of the Mission of the Church of the Nazarene* (Kansas City: Nazarene, 1973), 82.

64   Mildred Bangs Wynkoop, *John Wesley: Christian Revolutionary* (Kansas City: Beacon Hill, 1970), 14-15.

65   Cunningham, et al, *Our Watchword and Song*, 583-584.

66   See R. Franklin Cook and Stephen Weber, *The Greening: The Story of Nazarene Compassionate Ministries* (Kansas City: Nazarene, 1986).

67   *Herald of Holiness*, July 1, 1984, 4, 20; Al Truesdale and Steve Weber, eds., *Evangelism and Social Redemption: Addresses from a Conference on Compassionate Ministry*, November 1985 (Kansas City: Beacon Hill, 1987).

68   Neville Bartle, "Culture and the Beauty of Holiness: Reflections from the South Pacific," in *The Challenge of Culture: Articulating and Proclaiming the Wesleyan-Holiness Message in the Asia Pacific Region: Papers Presented at the Asia-Pacific Region 2001 Theology Conference*, ed. David Ackerman (Taytay, Rizal, Philippines: Asia-Pacific Nazarene Theological Seminary, 2002), 106.

69   Bresee, "The Glory of a Transcendent Purpose," 1903, in *Sayings of the Founder*, comp. Ward B. Chandler (Houston: Chandler and Roach, [1951]), 51.

70   Reynolds, *World-Wide Missions* (Kansas City: Nazarene, 1915).

71   A. J. Smith, *Jesus Lifting Chinese: Marvelous Spiritual Awakenings in China* (Cincinnati: God's Bible School and Revivalist, n.d.), 26.

72   Smith, *Jesus Lifting*, 36.

73   See Cunningham, *Holiness Abroad*, 159.

74   For example, see Reynolds, "Around the World Trip," to the General Missionary Board of the Pentecostal Church of the Nazarene [1914], Nazarene Archives.

75   J. Glenn Gould, *Missionary Pioneers and Our Debt to Them* (Kansas City: Nazarene, [1935]), 39.

76   Jones, "Our Foreign Policy," *Other Sheep*, January 1955, 3.

77   Bronell Greer, "Nazarene Troika," mimeographed [1969], Part Three, "Evangelism and the Evangelist," 31-32.

78   C. J. Kinne, *The Modern Samaritan: A Presentation of the Claims of Medical Missions* (Kansas City: Nazarene, n.d.), 10, 28, 85.

79   Williamson, "Will Democracy Live?" sermon (file 1234-1, Nazarene Archives).

80   Williamson, *Preaching Scriptural Holiness* (Kansas City: Beacon Hill, 1953), 49.

81   Hynd, "The Healing Urge of the Church," in *For the Healing of the Nations*, 72-73.

82   Betty Howard, *Why This Road: The Carolyn Myatt Story* (Kansas City: Nazarene, 2009). See Carol J. Bett, "The Influence of Social Capital on Community-Based Health Care Programs in Rural Papua New Guinea: An Ethnographic Study," PhD dissertation, U. of New Mexico, 2015.

83   "Missionary Questionairre," file 679-17, Nazarene Archives.

84 "The Start of Our Work in Brava," Folios for History of the Foreign Missionary Work of the Church of the Nazarene," [1921], 262-56, Nazarene Archives.

85 Rebecca Krikorian, *Jerusalem: The Life Sketch of Miss Rebecca Krikorian and Her Nephew Rev. Samuel Krikorian Together with Their Divine Call to Open a Field of Work in Jerusalem* (Kansas City: General Foreign Missionary Board, 1919). See Amy N. Hinshaw, *Messengers of the Cross in Palestine, Japan, and Other Islands* (Kansas City: Woman's Foreign Missionary Society, n.d.), 7-16, 21-23, 85-90.

86 Santin to Missionary Board, August 15, 1918, file 390-19.

87 H. T. Reza, *Washed by the Blood: Stories of Native Workers Connected with the Ministry of the Church of the Nazarene in the Mexican Field* (Kansas City: Beacon Hill, 1953), 17. See various correspondence of V. G. Santin, Nazarene Archives.

88 "Policy of the General Board to Govern Its Work in Foreign Fields," *Proceedings of the Church of the Nazarene: First to Eighth Sessions, October 1 to 4, 1923; Ninth to Thirty-third Sessions, December 4 to 14, 1923*, 63-64; also see file 305-15, Nazarene Archives.

89 Louise Robinson Chapman, *Footprints in Africa* (Kansas City: Nazarene, 1959), 39.

90 Amy N. Hinshaw, *Native Torch Bearers* (Kansas City: Nazarene, 1934), 152-170.

91 Cunningham, *Holiness Abroad*, 160-172.

92 *Proceedings of the Second General Assembly of the Pentecostal Church of the Nazarene*, ed. Robert Pierce (Los Angeles: Nazarene Publishing Company, [1908]). Mary Lee Cagle, *Life and Work of Mary Lee Cagle* (Kansas City: Nazarene, [1928]), includes a sermon on "Woman's Right to Preach," 160-176.

93 For the work of Elizondo and Garcia see Amy Hinshaw, *Native Torch Bearers* (Kansas City: Nazarene, 1934), 181-184, and 189-195; Stan Ingersol, "The Ties that Bind, Part 2," *Herald of Holiness* (November 15, 1988), 11; Ingersol, "Knowledge and Vital Piety: Lucia de Costas's Enduring Witness," *Herald of Holiness* (April 1996), 13; and Mae McReynolds Profile file, Nazarene Archives.

94 Betty Emslie, *With Both Hands: The Story of Mary Cooper of Gazaland* (Kansas City: Nazarene, 1970), Lorraine Schultz, *Only One Life: The Autobiography of Lorraine Schultz* (Kansas City; Nazarene, 1997); Marilyn Willis, "The People's Church," *World Mission* (November 1998), 3-4. Tshambe's son, Filimao Chambo, became a General Superintendent of the Church of the Nazarene in 2017.

95 *Nazarene Communication News* (March 17, 2007).

96 Helen Temple, *Adventure with God: The Jeanine van Beek Story* (Kansas City: Nazarene, 2002).

97 See C. S. Cowles, *A Woman's Place? Leadership in the Church* (Kansas City: Beacon Hill, 1993).

98 C. Warren Jones, *Look on the Fields* (Kansas City: Nazarene, 1950), 91. See Missionary Policy: Department of Foreign Missions, *General Board, Church of the Nazarene* (Kansas City: n.p., 1951), 5-6, 46-48; See also Hardy C.

Powers, "The Church at Home and Abroad," *Herald of Holiness*, March 12, 1952, 3; Benner, "The 'Go' in the Gospel," in *For the Healing of the Nations: Ten Missionary Sermons,* comp. C. Warren Jones (Kansas City: Beacon Hill, 1954), 50.

99 *Manual/Church of the Nazarene* 1997-2001, 252.

100 In Stan Ingersol, "The Inherent Tension in Nazarene Education," *Herald of Holiness*, April 15, 1989, 9.

101 Ronald Kirkemo, *For Zion's Sake: A History of Pasadena/Point Loma College* (San Diego: Point Loma Press, 1992), 8.

102 The Commission on Education presented a report adopted by the General Board in June 1952.

103 Philosophy of Education (1952).

104 DeLong and Taylor, *Fifty Years of Nazarene Missions*, vol. 2: *History of the Fields* (Kansas City: Beacon Hill, 1955), 183.

105 See, e.g., Hilario Pena, "Spanish Bible and Missionary Training Institute," *Other Sheep*, August 1947, 5.

106 Esselstyn, *Nazarene Missions in South Africa* (Kansas City: Nazarene, 1952), 78-90.

107 G. B. and Audrey Williamson, *Yesu Masiki Jay: A First Hand Survey of Nazarene Missionary Progress in India* (Kansas City: Beacon Hill, 1952), 65-66.

108 Mildred Bangs Wynkoop, "Educational Problems in Japan," April 1963, 22 pp., file 1387-74, Nazarene Archives.

109 Heard at http://ia600501.us.archive.org/8/items/SERMONINDEX_SID23702/SID23702.mp3.The following comments are loosely, not strictly, based on Benner's sermon.

GLOSSARY

amillennialism / amillennialist — see *millennialism.*

backslidden — when a Christian lapses into a pre-Christian state; to turn away from God and "fall away" from the faith.

cardinal doctrine — a belief that is foundational to a specific religious group.

carnality / carnal — associated with the passions and desires of the body that are expressed in unholy ways. It also is used to signify something that is secular, non-spiritual, or worldly.

contemplative monk — members of Roman Catholic religious orders who live in monasteries or convents shut off from the world in order to devote themselves completely to prayer, both prayer with others and personal prayer. In addition to prayer, the life of the contemplative monk or nun includes manual work, hours of silence, and study.

contextualisation — the process of interpreting biblical studies and theology so that they are meaningful in a specific culture.

ecumenism / ecumenical — promoting unity among Christian groups.

episcopacy — an organization governed by bishops.

formalism — rigidly adhering to prescribed ways of conducting worship services.

Fundamentalist camp — See *Fundamentalist-Modernist controversy*

Fundamentalist-Modernist controversy — a major schism among Protestants in the United States during the 1920s and 1930s. Based upon a particular view of biblical authority, Fundamentalism reacted against trends in Protestant circles that emphasized the superiority of reason as compared to Scripture. While Modernists emphasized the human composition of the Bible, Fundamentalists held that God himself had dictated the Bible, that every word of the original writings was composed by God, and that the Bible was, consequently, without any error. Interpreting Genesis's account of creation literally, Fundamentalists rejected evolution. Fundamentalists were pre-millennial. They viewed the world pessimistically, as becoming worse and worse. Christ would come again upon the fulfilment of biblical prophecies. Moderate modernists, who stressed religious experience as well as reason, won or retained control in major religious groups and theological schools. This led to divisions, especially in Presbyterian and Baptist denominations.

Great Depression — a severe, worldwide economic downturn in the 1930s.

Holiness movement — emerging from 19th-century Methodism, this phrase described a loosely associated groups of individuals, churches, schools, and organizations that emphasized the personal experience of entire sanctification, often called "the second work of grace." **The Wesleyan-Holiness movement** is a branch that distinguishes itself from the more Pentecostal forms of the Holiness movement.

Holiness revivalism — see *"revivalism"*

indigenisation / indigenous — making something more appropriate for a local culture, especially the use of more individuals from the culture in administration and employment.

individualism — a particular focus on the worth of each individual person rather than the community or collective.

Methodism — a general term used to describe a related group of activities, churches, and organizations deriving their inspiration from the life and teachings of John Wesley, George Whitefield, and Charles Wesley.

millennialist / millennialism — teachings about the future of humankind as it relates to the thousand-year reign of Christ mentioned in Revelation 20 and marked by the reality of peace justice across the earth. Premillennialism teaches that Christ will return to earth before the 1,000 years. Postmillennialism teaches that Christ will return after the church has effectively evangelized the whole world. Amillennialism teaches that the 1,000 years are symbolic and that we are already living in God's reign. Dispensationalism is a form of premillennialism that teaches that Christ will return in two stages: the rapture (where believers dead and alive are taken into heaven) followed by a public revelation several years later at which point the 1,000 years will begin.

Modernist camp — See *Fundamentalist-Modernist controversy*

Nicene Creed — written in 325 AD, it is the statement of belief that is most widely accepted by Christian churches worldwide.

orthodox, orthodoxy, orthodox theology — doctrines, theories, and practices that are generally accepted by most Christians. This is not to be confused with the Orthodox Church, which is a particular, Christian denomination.

polity — the government and rules that shape a specific organizations identity and practices.

post-millennialist / pre-millennial — see *millennialism*

prevenient grace — the actions of God at work in people's lives before they make a decision about salvation. See *preventing grace.*

preventing grace — a phrase that Wesley used to speak about the actions of God that spark hope in the human heart for deliverance from sin and return to God. See *prevenient grace.*

Revivalism / Holiness revivalism — beginning among Protestants in America around the turn of the nineteenth century, and spreading throughout the world. Revivalists (evangelists) encouraged and pleaded with persons to recognize their sin, to avail of grace, to believe in Christ with their whole selves, to repent, to make genuine commitments to Christ, and, thus, to be saved. In contrast to strict Calvinism, which emphasized that only the elect would be saved, revivalism offered salvation to all. To any who heard the gospel, God gave grace enough to be saved, but a person must respond in favour of that grace. In holiness revivalism, evangelists beckoned believers toward heart-holiness or entire sanctification. In both cases, revivalism was attached to camp meetings, evangelistic crusades, and special services in local churches. Historically, revivalism asked persons to make commitments to Christ by coming forward at the end of a sermon, typically, during a song, to bow and to pray at a kneeling rail, called an "altar," in the front of the sanctuary. When Christians were so formed, revivalists believed, society could be changed.

scholasticism — an emphasis within various religious groups, both Roman Catholic and Protestant, upon the right confession of faith and the rational or intellectual side of faith. Possessing right doctrine, as constructed by reason on the basis of the Bible and the teaching of the Church, is of utmost concern. In scholasticism, belief is an individual's assent or agreement with the doctrines of the Church. Scholasticism tends toward rigidity in theology.

Wesleyan-holiness movement — See *Holiness Movement*

FRAMEWORKS FOR LAY LEADERSHIP

ABOUT THE EDITOR

Rob A. Fringer, PhD–Principal and lecturer in Biblical Studies and Biblical Language at Nazarene Theological College in Brisbane. Rob is an ordained elder in the Church of the Nazarene and has 15 years of pastoral experience working in the areas of Youth, Adult Discipleship, and Community Outreach. He is co-author of *Theology of Luck: Fate, Chaos, & Faith* and *The Samaritan Project* both published by Beacon Hill Press of Kansas City. Rob is married (Vanessa) and has two children (Sierra and Brenden).

BOOKS IN THE
FRAMEWORKS FOR LAY LEADERSHIP SERIES

ENGAGING THE STORY OF GOD
Rob A. Fringer

EXPLORING A WESLEYAN THEOLOGY
David B. McEwan

EMBODYING A THEOLOGY OF MINISTRY AND LEADERSHIP
Bruce G. Allder

ENTERING THE MISSION OF GOD
Richard Giesken

EXPRESSING A NAZARENE IDENTITY
Floyd Cunningham

EMBRACING A DOCTRINE OF HOLINESS
David B. McEwan and Rob A. Fringer